THE CYCLIST'S COMPANION

George Theohari

A THINK BOOK

Whoever invented the bicycle deserves the thanks of humanity.
Lord Charles Beresford

THINK
BOOKS

First published in Great Britain in 2007 by
Think Publishing
The Pall Mall Deposit
124-128 Barlby Road, London W10 6BL
www.thinkpublishing.co.uk

Distributed in the UK and Ireland by Macmillan Distribution Ltd,
Brunel Road, Houndmills, Basingstoke RG21 6XS

Distributed in the United States and Canada by
Sterling Publishing Co Inc,
387 Park Avenue South
New York, NY 10016-8810

Text © Pan Macmillan Ltd
Design and layout © Think Publishing 2007
The moral rights of the author have been asserted

Author: George Theohari
Editor: Jo Swinnerton
Companion team: Tania Adams, James Collins, Rica Dearman,
Lauren Goddard, Emma Jones, Richard Rees, Mark Searle
and Marion Thompson

ISBN-13: 978-1-84525-049-2

Printed in the UK by Mackays of Chatham

I thought of that while riding my bike.
Albert Einstein, on the theory of relativity

THANKS TO

The esteemed officers of CTC, the UK's national cyclists' organisation, who allowed me to pick their bike-nut brains, particularly Matt Mallinder, Chris Juden, Kevin Mayne, Mark Waters, Cherry Allan, Yannick Read, Ian Warby;

Monica Ory and Carole Jones at the National Cycle Archive at Warwick University, for helping me dig for treasure;

Deborah and Saul for their love, patience and understanding in the face of unrelenting cyclemania;

Angela and Maria, Margaret and Rick, who worked as hard as any *domestiques* to help me over the cols and into the perfect sprint finish.

Cycling at 12mph equates to 3mph walking. Each takes about 75 watts of power from the 'human engine' – just one of a myriad facts contained within this compact tome. A fact that goes a long way to explaining both the joys and benefits of cycling. Simply, like this *Companion*, it makes sense. That is not to say that there's not a whiff of nonsense here, too. For example, the longest bike ever ridden measured more than 28m and was ridden in the Netherlands for a distance of 100m in 2002.

This is a delightful Think Book, packed with all the information about bikes and biking you need to know, never knew you needed to know, and perhaps thought you didn't need to know anyway.

Cyclists have always had an air of eccentricity about them and this book is a neat accompaniment for such a condition. Particularly for those of us who seek to proselytise on behalf of cycling, these pages leave us well armed. From health benefits to world records, it's all here.

No cyclist's life is complete without this *Companion*, and anyone who isn't a cyclist will be seriously persuaded to become one by merely leafing through its pages. Enjoy!

Jon Snow, newscaster, cyclist and CTC President

TWO WHEELS GOOD, FOUR WHEELS BAD

These figures show just how easy it would be, in most cases, to leave the motor at home and jump in the saddle instead.

22% of all trips are under 1 mile
41% of all trips are under 2 miles
68% of all trips are under 5 miles

23% of car driver trips are under 2 miles
56% of car driver trips are under 5 miles

54% of bicycle trips are under two miles, and the average bicycle trip length is 2.4 miles

Source: Sustrans

QUOTE UNQUOTE

Cycle tracks will abound in Utopia.
HG Wells, author, *A Modern Utopia*

BICYCLE PERKS

Many UK employers run tax-break schemes that allow staff to save up to 50% on the retail price of a new machine.

But some organisations have gone much further in a bid to boost their eco-friendly credentials and encourage workers to stay fit, healthy and happy.

Here are some of the most impressive examples of pro-cyclist largesse so far:

Ikea (UK) – For Christmas 2006, the UK arm of Ikea gave free folding bikes to all its 9,000 workers.

Google (Europe/Africa) – In early 2007, the internet firm issued staff in Europe, Africa and the Middle East with a catalogue from which to choose free bikes and kit.

Dahon (US) – The folding bicycle maker gives free cycles to any employee at its California HQ who cycles to work at least three times a week.

Worcestershire County Council (UK) – A special case, as the authority's offer of free bikes on loan applies not only to its own workers, but also to those in all local businesses. Employees can use a bike at no cost for three months and at the end of the loan period they can either return the bike or purchase it for £100.

POPULAR LONG-DISTANCE CYCLE ROUTES IN ENGLAND

Camel Trail

The Camel Trail, in Cornwall, accommodates 350,000 users each year. The 17-mile (largely traffic-free) cycleway passes through some of the most spectacular countryside in the south-west. It follows the course of a disused railway line along the Camel Estuary from Padstow to Wadebridge, before cutting through the deeply incised and beautifully wooded Camel Valley to Bodmin. At Bodmin, the trail winds its way inland to the foot of Bodmin Moor where it comes to an end near Blisland, a famously pretty moorland village.

TOP 10 BIKE RIDES IN THE WORLD

As selected by The Guardian, *January 2007*
Alpe d'Huez, France
Langkawi, Malaysia
Dubois, Wyoming, to Grand Teton National Park, US
Port Phillip Bay, Melbourne, Australia
Jotunheimen National Park, Norway
Uyuni salt flat, Bolivia
Highway 12 from Lolo Pass to Lowell, Idaho, US
Gorges de la Jonte, Cevennes, France
Whitehaven to Sunderland, UK
London to Hever Castle, Kent, UK

BABEL CYCLE

Some foreign words for 'bicycle'

Czech	*kolo*
Dutch	*fiets*
French	*bicyclette*
German	*fahrrad*
Greek	*podilato*
Irish	*rothar*
Italian	*bicicletta*
Polish	*rower*
Russian	*velociped*
Spanish	*bicicleta*
Swedish	*cykel*
Turkish	*bisiklet*

WRITERS ON BICYCLES

The great limbs of the athlete made the heavy machine spring and quiver with every stroke, while the mignon grey figure with the laughing face, and the golden curls blowing from under the little pin-banded straw hat, simply held firmly to her perch, and let the treadles whirl round beneath her feet. Mile after mile they flew, the wind beating in her face, the trees dancing past in two long ranks on either side, until they had passed round Croydon, and were approaching Norwood once more from the further side.

Arthur Conan Doyle, *Beyond the City,* **1892**

VELOCIO'S SEVEN COMMANDMENTS

Paul de Vivie, aka Velocio (1853-1930), publisher of *Le Cycliste*, was an early champion of the derailleur gear system and is regarded as the father of French bicycle touring and randonneuring (long-distance endurance rides).

1. Keep your rest short and infrequent to maintain your rhythm.

2. Eat before you are hungry and drink before you are thirsty.

3. Never ride to the point of exhaustion where you can't eat or sleep.

4. Cover up before you are cold, peel off before you are hot.

5. Don't drink, smoke or eat meat on tour.

6. Never force the pace, especially during the first hours.

7. Never ride just for the sake of riding.

CROWD TROUBLE

At the 2005 Druivencross, one of the biggest cyclo-cross events in Belgium, Bart Wellens kicked a spectator who had been abusing him throughout the race before crossing the line in first position. 'For four laps, I had mud and beer thrown at me,' Wellens told a Belgian cycling website shortly afterwards. 'The fifth time it was just too much for me. I didn't really intend to hit him, and I regret what I've done, but I think that as a rider I don't have to put up with everything.' The race jury allowed the victory to stand, but the Union Cycliste Internationale later stripped Wellens of his title.

COMMUTER TIME TRIAL

Results of a contest between different forms of transport, staged by *The Guardian* in London, showed just how efficient cycling can be. The route was a typical commuter stretch of 6.5 miles through the capital: from Muswell Hill in the north via Crouch End, Holloway, Islington, Farringdon and Ludgate Circus, ending up at St Paul's Cathedral. The trip takes 45 minutes by bus.

RESULTS

Motorcycle
Time: 24 min
Average speed: 16.2mph
Fuel consumption: 49mpg
Make: Yamaha XT600
Price: £4,189

Bicycle
Time: 27 min
Average speed: 14.4mph
Fuel consumption: nil
Make: Specialized
Price: £350

Car
Time: 44 min
Average speed: 8.8mph
Fuel consumption: 28mpg
Make: Honda Civic ESi
Price: £12,845

GARDENING RISKIER THAN CYCLING

Who would have thought it? We all know the daily risks that face road cyclists whenever they mount their bikes – from potholes to oil slicks to erratic drivers – but, according to one recent study published in *The Sydney Morning Herald*, they are better off messing about in the saddle than the soil.

Around 5% of gardeners – compared to 4% of cyclists – were found to require medical care for an injury related to their respective activity. Although the study did not touch on the dangers arising from a combination of the two hobbies, it would be safe to assume that attempting to prune a tall rose while standing on one's bicycle seat is to be avoided at all costs.

Just how big was the first cycling boom? AC Pemberton, in the 1897 handbook *The Complete Cyclist*, captures the excitement surrounding the new craze, as well as neatly summing up its unprecedented effect on British society and industry:

'For nearly 20 years, the cycle had been among us in daily use with its immense capabilities fully proved, before the general public realised its powers. The riders were in the minority, and society refused to look upon it with the slightest favour. It was not until the year 1895 that cycling became fashionable as well as popular. Then ladies began to take it up, and the depots of the large manufacturers on Holborn Viaduct were choked by crowds of "smart" people, all anxious to secure machines. Trade waxed fat for the manufacturers... but the actual demand that was to follow during 1896 surpassed the wildest dreams of the most sordid owner of cycling plant.

'...Steel tubes were at famine prices; makers found themselves short of all the components which they did not themselves manufacture... Tales are told of men wandering round London seeking for machines, and only finding them at a premium of something like 40% over the usual price. In the midlands, masters and workmen deserted trades they had followed all their lives to become either manufacturers or to be employed in the industry.

'...America appears to have been before us in having its boom, and, when the tales of the prosperity of the trade in England reached that country, the manufacturers who had found themselves overstocked were not slow to take advantage of a market already made for their wares. As is the custom with the Yanks, they did not do things by halves. Depots were taken in London in the best and most expensive situations, and money was spent freely in advertising in more original and attractive methods than had been the custom with English cycle makers, who had from long security grown to imagine that their manufactures were of such unimpeachable quality that nothing could jeopardise their position as makers to the whole world. At first they pooh-poohed the fact that anyone would have the audacity to compete with them on their own ground.

'...But the handsome appearance of the American machines, combined with their light weight – which, taken as an average, was several pounds below that of the best English cycles as supplied to the ordinary public – made them at once favourites, and it is quite possible that in future years the machine made in America will largely share the home market.'

14 *The percentage by which the average distance cycled by bike owners in the UK dropped between 1980 and 2002, from 44 to 38 miles a year*

OLD PICTURE, NEW CAPTION

GEOGRAPHY:
A DONEGAL TOURING MEMORY.

Arthur rued his luck. Once more, the only person he could find to ask directions turned out to be illiterate and drunk.

QUOTE UNQUOTE

The bicycle is just as good company as most husbands and, when it gets old and shabby, a woman can dispose of it and get a new one without shocking the entire community.
Ann Strong, journalist, *Minneapolis Tribune*

BULLFIGHTERS ON BICYCLES

Unruly canines are a common cause of complaint among cyclists, particularly those that lie in wait at the top of French hill roads, hoping for a taste of Lycra-covered flesh.

But next time you wobble at the sight of a jumping dog, spare a thought for the bull-baiting wheelmen who, according to a 1896 report of the Cyclists' Touring Club's (as CTC was then called) monthly gazette, taunted 'Toro' from the top of their penny farthings – and lived to tell the tale: 'All the bullfighters were cyclists and mounted on bicycles for the fray. Reports say it was a complete success – from the cyclist's point of view.'

RIDING RIDDLES

Who is this famous cyclist?
BRAHMSIAN CORD

Answer on page 151.

THEY ARE THE CHAMPIONS

Multiple Tour de France winners

Rider	Number of wins
Lance Armstrong	7
Jacques Anquetil	5
Bernard Hinault	5
Miguel Induráin	5
Eddy Merckx	5
Louison Bobet	3
Greg Lemond	3
Phillippe Thys	3
Gino Bartali	2
Ottavio Bottecchia	2
Fausto Coppi	2
Laurent Fignon	2
Nicholas Frantz	2
Firmin Lambot	2
André Leducq	2
Sylvere Maes	2
Antonin Magne	2
Lucien Petit-Breton	2
Bernard Thevenet	2

MUSICAL INSPIRATION

Great Britain team cyclist Craig MacLean, a keen guitarist as well as one of the world's fastest riders over a lap of the track, gets his blood boiling before races by listening to hard rock music on headphones while warming up. Here are his top five playlist picks:

1. **Motörhead** 'Ace of Spades'
2. **Foo Fighters** 'Monkey Wrench'
3. **The Sex Pistols** 'Anarchy in the UK'
4. **Metallica** 'Blitzkrieg'
5. **Led Zeppelin** 'Custard Pie'

16 *Age of Tessie Reynolds when, in 1893, she caused a sensation by riding from London to Brighton and back in a 'trousered costume'*

CYCLING CAVEATS

Thou shalt have no other riders before thee
If you see a rider in the distance, no matter how far ahead or on what kind of bike, you must chase them down. You are the greyhound, they are the hare.

Thou shalt not make unto thee any graven image
There has been much debate about this commandment and with time it passed into desuetude, to the extent that between the years of 1927 and 1996 the commandments were known as the nine commandments. And then Halfords started selling cheap full-suspension mountain bikes.

Thou shalt take the frame on board in train
Beware the zealot who stops you embarking, as he is an emissary of evil and you must do all in your power to combat him.

Remember the repair kit, to keep the tyre from being holy
You might go months, even years, without a puncture, but don't be suckered into over confidence. They're waiting. Just around the next corner.

Honour thy bicycle and thy bike shop
Breakages are an unfortunate inevitability. But honouring thy bike will keep them to a minimum, and honouring thy bike shop will cut down on troubles when they do happen.

Thou shalt not fall
Falling off is not fun. There's that moment where you realise you're going to come off – the point... where your brain tells your body that, sorry, but this is going to sting a little bit.

Thou shalt not commit Moultonery
It's just wrong. It looks like a folder, it's the right size and shape, with strange thin webbing-like tubing, and yet, when you come to fold it up, you simply can't.

Though shalt not ride on the pavement
But you will won't you? And Gladys will write to the local paper exclaiming that all cyclists should be given the birch.

Thou shalt not bear false fitness against thy neighbour
When with friends, do not... tell them you haven't been out for a while and might struggle to keep up, only to drop everyone on the first incline.

Thou shalt covet thy neighbour's bikes
No matter how much you don't want your jealousy to show you will always let slip a slight whistle of satisfaction... or a mutter of 'nice bike' to which the recipient... will accept graciously and carry on his way with a warm glow.

Anthony Robson, *The Ten Commandments of Cycling*, www.citycycling.co.uk

WRITERS ON BICYCLES

He dropped down the hills on his bicycle. The roads were greasy, so he had to let it go. He felt a pleasure as the machine plunged over the second, steeper drop in the hill. 'Here goes!' he said. It was risky, because of the curve in the darkness at the bottom, and because of the brewers' waggons with drunken waggoners asleep. His bicycle seemed to fall beneath him, and he loved it. Recklessness is almost a man's revenge on his woman. He feels he is not valued, so he will risk destroying himself to deprive her altogether.

DH Lawrence, *Sons and Lovers*, 1913

CLUB RULES

The correct way to behave on the road, as laid out in a Bicycle Touring Club (now CTC) circular, 1880:

- Members shall keep as much as possible to the left or near side of the road.
- It is illegal to ride on any path set aside for foot passengers, and this practice should be entirely avoided.
- The Rules of the Road should be most strictly followed out. Thus (a) in meeting, keep to the left and (b) in overtaking, pass on the right. But led horses must always be met and passed on the side on which the man in charge is. NB In every civilised country except Great Britain Rules (a) and (b) are reversed, and you meet on the right and pass on the left.
- Before passing a vehicle or foot-passenger, notice should be given at a sufficient distance by whistle, bell or otherwise.
- Never pass between two vehicles or riders when you are over-taking them.
- If any rider or vehicle wishes to pass you, keep well over to the left.
- Special care should be taken in turning corners, especially where a full view of the road is not obtainable.
- It is considered advisable to avoid, as much as possible, the use of the voice when passing foot-passengers or vehicles.
- In meeting or passing restive horses a dismount should only be made if requested, as sudden dismounts often have the worst effect. A slow pace, and a few words, form the best course. The rider should always keep as far away from the horse as possible.
- Riders should not take the ground in front of a horse until at least 10 yards ahead.

18 *Average number of cyclists in thousands who entered London's congestion zone each day in May and June 2003*

BRAND VALUES

Approximate cycle sales in the UK 2005 by brand, per unit

Universal (inc Muddy Fox) 600,000
Raleigh 400,000
Concept 385,000
Halfords' own labels 355,000
Moore Large 228,000
Vega 200,000
Professional 180,000
Falcon 125,000
Giant 117,000
MV Sport .... 88,000+
Trek 75,000
Claud Butler/Shogun 75,000
Specialized 72,000
Saracen 60,000
Cycle Citi 60,000
Boss/Townsend/Coventry Eagle 55,000
Optima 55,000
Reece 50,000
Avocet 46,000
Dawes 32,000
Mongoose 32,000
GT 30,000
Ridgeback 25,000
Scott 24,000
Marin 21,000
Brompton 19,000
Kona 18,000
Pashley 10,000
Cannondale 10,000
Dahon 9,000
Powabyke 5,000
DDG 4,000
Orange 2,800
Norco 1,200
Whyte 950
Others .... 100,000+
TOTAL .... **3,569,950+**

Source: BikeBiz, 2006

*Number of years for which Swiss cyclist Oscar Egg held the record for 19
cycling 44.247km in one hour, accomplished in 1914*

BICYCLE THEFT HOTSPOTS

A guide to English districts with the most number of bike thefts in one year (2005-2006), with the average value of claims for stolen bikes in parentheses.

1. London (£342.58)
2. Kingston-upon-Thames (£420.03)
3. Cambridge (£221.82)
4. Bristol (£360.26)
5. York (£299.04)
6. Oxford (£295.65)
7. Richmond & Twickenham (£321.51)
8. Brighton (£361.21)
9. Portsmouth (£249.74)
10. Nottingham (£257.91)

QUOTE UNQUOTE

Just as the ideal of classic Greek culture was the most perfect harmony of mind and body, so a human and a bicycle are the perfect synthesis of body and machine.
Richard Ballantine, author, *Richard's Ultimate Bicycle Book*

DID FASCISTS KILL OTTAVIO BOTTECCHIA?

Ottavio Bottecchia was the first Italian to win the Tour de France; he held the jersey from start to finish in 1924, and was victor again in 1925. Not bad for a former bricklayer from Umbria who took up professional cycling after serving in the Italian army during World War I.

His run of early successes soon established him as a national hero in his home country, where he became known as *le maçon de Frioul* (the mason from Frioul), but he did not enjoy his fame for long. In June 1927, he was murdered while out training. He was found at the roadside, near a vineyard, with bruises and a serious skull fracture. His bicycle was undamaged, propped against a nearby tree.

The official cause of death was sunstroke; given the circumstances in which he was found, one can see why other theories have taken root. The most prominent is that Bottecchia, an outspoken socialist and extremely popular, was taken out because he was an embarrassment to the Fascist government of Mussolini.

Guess the bicycle-related solution to this puzzle

Wheelman rages uphill a little easier with these.

Answer on page 151.

BABY, WE WERE BORN TO RIDE

In January 2006, *Bicycling* magazine rated the best 21 cities for cycling in North America. Portland, the overall winner, also topped the last such survey carried out by the magazine, in 2001.

The choices were based on factors including cycling-friendly statistics (numbers of bike lanes and routes, number of bike racks, and city bike projects completed and planned), bike culture (number of bike commuters, popular clubs, cycling events and renowned bike shops), and climate/geography (the quality of roads and trails for riding, and how frequently Mother Nature lets riders enjoy them).

Best US Cycling City (overall):
   Portland, OR

Best Cycling City (population 1 million or more):
   1. San Diego, CA
   2. Chicago, IL
   3. New York, NY
   Honourable mention: Philadelphia, PA; Phoenix, AZ

Best Cycling City (population 500,000 to 1 million):
   1. Portland, OR
   2. Denver, CO
   3. Seattle, WA
   Honourable mention: San Francisco, CA; Austin, TX

Best Cycling City (population 200,000 to 500,000):
   1. Madison, WI
   2. Tucson, AZ
   3. Albuquerque, NM
   Honourable mention: Minneapolis, MN; Anchorage, AK

Best Cycling City (population 75,000 to 200,000)
   1. Boulder, CO
   2. Eugene, OR
   3. Ann Arbor, MI
   Honourable mention: Chattanooga, TN; Cambridge, MA

Best Small Town for Cycling: Davis, CA (population 60,308)

CYCLE COUTURE

Armani

At the end of the Paris Fashion Show in 2005, Giorgio Armani unveiled the fruits of his partnership with Italian bike maker Bianchi: the Emporio Armani Sportbike. Male models rode out onto the catwalk on sleek, jet-black hybrids that would later go on sale through Armani stores. Modish tweaks to this flat-handlebar, hybrid 'leisure and training' bike included an iPod holder and a fabric bottle-cage, both featuring the Armani logo (which is also emblazoned on the frame).

The involvement of Bianchi, one of the world's most respected producers, ensured the Sportbike went beyond a mere fashion novelty, with the inclusion of Shimano components and a lightweight aluminium frame. A matching pair were reportedly given as wedding gifts to Tom Cruise and Katie Holmes, close friends of Mr Armani.

Perhaps this well-thought-out fashion bike proved more desirable than the designer might have anticipated, though – on the very day that the first bike went on display in the Armani store at Caesars Palace, Las Vegas, it was snatched and ridden away by a fashion-conscious thief. Richard Stroem of Bianchi said at the time: 'That's the only bike of that type in the world, so if that guy is riding his bike, they will know it's stolen.'

BEST BMX

The estimated sales figures for quality BMX bikes in the UK

Mongoose	20,000
GT	15,000
Haro	12,000
Diamondback	5,000
Ruption/Huffy	5,000
Others	5,000

HEY, BIG SPENDERS

A survey in the UK's Peak District National Park found that cyclists holidaying in the park spent an average of £25 per person per day. The average spend of visitors arriving by car or other forms of transport was £7.30 a day. This is because cyclists tend to shop locally, whereas drivers can buy in a lot of their provisions in advance and carry them in the car.

Artistic cycling

Artistic cycling – a highly choreographed combination of cycling and gymnastics set to music – is relatively unknown in the UK, but it is highly popular in Germany, where there are no fewer than 10,000 licence-holding participants, according to the International Union of Cyclists.

The main annual event is the artistic cycling World Championships (first held in 1956). Competitors, entering as individuals or in pairs, perform before judges in six-minute rounds by singles, pairs and four- or six-man teams. The display – which can include stands, jumps, turns, wheelies, stops and more – must be executed within a small area on a wooden court, marked by painted lines.

The bicycles used for artistic cycling are highly specialised: they feature a fixed-wheel transmission, with a one-to-one gearing ratio (where the sprocket and chainring are the same size). The wheels must be of equal size and are closely spaced in order to make tricks, such as wheelies, easier to perform. The handlebars look like inverted drop-handlebars and can be spun through 360 degrees.

DIY FOR CYCLISTS

Ten best-selling books about bike maintenance and techniques

1. *The Bike Book*, by Fred Milson
2. *Zinn and the Art of Mountain Bike Maintenance*, by Lennard Zinn
3. *Mountain Bike Like a Champion*, by Ned Overend and Ed Pavelka
4. *Your First Triathlon*, by Joe Friel
5. *Bicycling Magazine's Illustrated Bicycle Maintenance*, by Todd Downs
6. *Mastering Mountain Bike Skills*, by Brian Lopes and Lee McCormack
7. *The Lance Armstrong Performance Program*, by Lance Armstrong and Chris Carmichael
8. *Smart Cycling: Successful Training and Racing for Riders of All Levels*, by Arnie Baker
9. *Cyclecraft: Skilled Cycling Techniques for Adults*, by John Franklin
10. *Pocket Mountain Bike Maintenance – Repairs on the Road*, by Mel Allwood

The village of Ripley, at one time an important coaching stop on the London to Portsmouth Road, was known in the late 1900s as a mecca for good cyclists.

The main destination for wheelmen and women was the (still thriving) Anchor Hotel in the High Street. Cyclists' visitor books from the ramshackle, half-timbered hostelry, covering the period 1881-1895, are signed by as many as 7,000 riders a year. The books, stored in the archives of the Surrey History Centre, reveal that HG Wells was among the visitors.

The Ripley ride was such a widespread phenomenon that in 1896, it prompted toymakers J Jacques & Son to create a board game based on the 50-mile round journey from London. Wheeling ('a new and exciting game for cyclists') came complete with an illustrated board depicting the journey, detailed models of riders on bikes for counters, and a deck of 'accessory' cards featuring items such as lamps and bells to help players on their way.

St Mary's, the village church, has a stained glass window of Harriet and Annie Dibble, the sisters who ran the Anchor at the time and who made it so popular with cyclists, offering tea and Bible readings for travellers who were missing their usual Sunday service. The window was funded through a collection by grateful cyclists.

A contemporary account by AC Pemberton captures the excitement of the weekly pilgrimage to the Anchor, made by riders of ordinaries (penny-farthings) or boneshakers from far and wide. Pemberton noted in *The Complete Cyclist*, 1897: 'Probably the most classic highway on which all good cyclists are supposed at some time to make a pilgrimage is the old Portsmouth road; the portion as far as Ripley being a regular promenade on a Sunday morning.

'Thousands of wheelmen and women pass through Kingston every Sunday. They are to be seen mounted on all sorts and conditions of machines, from the latest inventor's fad to the ancient crock fast tumbling to pieces. The reason for the wonderful popularity of their stretch of road has to be traced back to the early ordinary days. Old Jack Keen, who was then the champion *par excellence*, discovered the Anchor at Ripley.

'Other well-known racing men followed his lead. The racing man was not in those days the professional as he is in these, and to be seen in his company was presumed to reflect some glory on the ordinary individual. Then the cycling clubs took up the road, and as there was at that time only one inn of which cyclists could be sure, all flocked to the Anchor.'

*Giles had discovered a foolproof way of resolving
arguments with careless motorists.*

*The bicycle is the most civilised conveyance known to man.
Other forms of transport grow daily more nightmarish.
Only the bicycle remains pure in heart.*
Iris Murdoch, author, *The Red and the Green*

EARLY CYCLING DITTIES

1915 Christmas Bulletin of the 2/6th Cycle Battalion
(Suffolk Regiment)
'Some Suffolk Worthies – Biographical Fragments' (excerpt)

A sporting young cyclist from Leiston,
Joined the Corps on a bike which he raced on;
One patrol cured his folly,
And now he's quite jolly
On a full roadster 'bus which weighs eight stone.

By 'HG' (believed to be Captain H Graves,
according to pencil mark)

QUOTE UNQUOTE

A bicycle hides nothing and threatens nothing. It is what it does,
its form is its function.
Stewart Parker, playwright, *Spokesong*

BOOZE, BREWS, BUT NO BIKES

It's hard to believe sometimes, but soap operas are generally supposed to reflect reality. Well, one area that they manage to accurately portray is the UK's indifference to pedal power; research carried out in 2007 found that bicycle use is virtually non-existent in telly land.

Researchers working for Cycling England, the national body charged by the government with turning more people into cyclists, watched hundreds of hours of the nation's favourite soaps over a four-week period, and reported that:

• Of the 95 characters to appear on screen, only two (Mickey from *EastEnders* and Amy from *Coronation Street*) were shown to own bikes.

• In total, lead characters were shown with bikes just four times, and one of these was a hit and run that left *EastEnders*' Stacey injured. Cycling extras appeared a couple more times: a total of six in *EastEnders*, and three in both *Coronation Street* and *Emmerdale*.

• There was not a cyclist to be seen among the youthful cast of *Hollyoaks* (even though under 16s in England own more than six million bikes). Not riding around on bikes did, however, allow the characters to focus on more traditional British pastimes: over a period of four weeks, its 20 or so cast members ordered 128 alcoholic drinks and made 54 cuppas.

Percentage of UK greenhouse gas emissions in 2002 caused by transport, in part due to people walking and cycling less and driving more

ONE SIZE DOES NOT FIT ALL

Wearing a cycle helmet that does not fit properly could double your chances of a head injury in the event of a crash, according to a study carried out in the US.

Researchers from the Harborview Injury Prevention and Research Centre (HIPRC) in Seattle questioned more than 1,700 cyclists of all ages who had worn a helmet when they were involved in a crash.

There were many accounts of helmets tilting backwards at the time of the crash or falling off altogether – 13% and 4% respectively. While a backwards tilt doubled the risk of a head injury, those that came off tripled the risk.

The 1999 study also compared head sizes and helmet measurements, and found that almost half of children who had sustained head injuries had helmets that were significantly wider than their heads – 2cm or more.

ALL TOGETHER NOW

Annual cycle sport events and numbers of cyclists taking part

Road racing: 2,101 events with 126,060 participants

Time trials: 1,932 events with 85,000 participants

MTB: 138 events with 20,700 participants

Cycle speedway: 373 events with 6,500 participants

Track: 383 events with 10,250 participants

BMX: 79 events with 8,000 participants

Cyclo cross: 210 events with 11,000 participants

(Source: British Cycling, 2002)

POPULAR LONG-DISTANCE CYCLE ROUTES IN ENGLAND

The Sustrans C2C

The Sustrans C2C (coast to coast) is the UK's most popular long-distance cycle route. It crosses England from the Irish Sea (Cumbrian coast) to the North Sea (Northumbrian coast), wending its way through the Lake District before climbing the Pennines ('the roof of England') then descending to the railway paths of County Durham. Highlights of the 140-mile ride include Black Hill, the highest point on the National Cycle Network at 609m, and the Consett-Sunderland railway path and sculpture trail.

In The Complete Cyclist *(AC Pemberton, 1897), Mrs F Harcourt Williamson records how high society – and in particular, its female constituents – helped to make cycling fashionable in Victorian England in the face of initial 'opprobrium':*

It was women who first made bicycling the fashion. At least 10 years before there was any idea of we women ever riding on wheels, the bicycle had made its way into popular favour as a useful and hygienic means of locomotion; but it might have been always confined to the business of the comparatively few instead of being applied to the pleasure of the many, if by some happy chance it had not been taken up by the right people and straightaway become the craze of the season, while it is well known that what once is approved by the classes will in the need be patronized also by the masses.

In the beginning the bicyclist was called – and for a time the title stuck – 'a cad on castors'. It was only a very few daring people who braved opprobrium, and made a convenience of the new machine. At a comparatively later date, clerks who lived out of London began to appreciate its uses, and after a time women (also engaged on business) were to be seen winding their way from the suburbs to the City.

Then the professional men began to use it a little, but still the exercise was condemned by the majority as vulgar; and – remembering how only a few years ago the appearance of a cyclist was greeted with derisive cheers, and how mischievous urchins took delight in throwing down their caps before a machine in the hopes of an upset; remembering too how adventurous women were almost mobbed upon their first appearance riding – it is difficult to realize that now all the royalties in Europe (except the Emperor of Germany, who is very dogged in his disapproval of the sport as suitable for ladies!) are patronizing the sport; and boys in red uniforms, with the name of 'Gavin' on their caps, may be seen waiting on the steps of Mayfair and Belgravia Mansions to clean the aristocracy's machines.

QUOTE UNQUOTE

The bicycle, the bicycle surely, should always be the vehicle of novelists and poets.
Christopher Morley, author, *Parnassus on Wheels*

---

28 *Date in June 1914 when the 12th Tour de France started – the same day that Archduke Ferdinand was shot, precipitating World War I*

OLD PICTURE, NEW CAPTION

The CREE
at Newton Stewart

*Stanley's advice to his wife to slow down before reaching the
bend had apparently gone unheeded.*

ACCIDENTS INVOLVING POTHOLES

If you've been involved in an accident caused by poorly maintained
roads, it is important to follow these steps in order to make a claim:

- Take names, telephone numbers and addresses of at least two
  witnesses where possible
- If injured, ensure that you seek medical advice
- Photograph the accident scene, including the pothole, and any
  personal injuries
- Do not inform the local authorities until photographic evidence
  has been collected of the scene and, if the accident is serious,
  the cause of the accident has been witnessed by police and/or
  your solicitor
- Pinpoint the pothole on CTC's reporting-site fillthathole.org.uk and
  the information will be passed on to the relevant local authority

TUNNEL VISION

Why are British cyclists being painted and stuck in a wind tunnel?

British track cycling is one of the success stories of recent years, with a run of medals in the Olympics and a reputation for constant innovation in training and development.

Dave Brailsford, British Cycling's performance director, is certainly not one to shy away from experimental – not to say bizarre – methods if he thinks it will knock a few micro-seconds off a rider's time.

So it is, then, that twice a year his team cyclists are painted from head to foot and placed in a wind tunnel in a bid to measure the effects of wind resistance on their performance. The reason? Paint separates on the skin where resistance is at its greatest.

RIDING RIDDLES

Who is this famous cyclist?
DONALD IS FLY
Answer on page 151.

THE AGE OF HEROES

Today's professional cyclists are, drug scandals aside, acknowledged as being among the toughest athletes in any sport. But, as any racing enthusiast over a certain age will tell you, nothing compares with the golden age of cycling, when courses were designed to be fiendishly difficult, and the men that rode them were true heroes.

Well, none of that has changed as far as the participants of L'Eroica ('heroic') are concerned. A unique event that combines a gruelling road race and period costume display, L'Eroica takes place every year in the Chianti region of Tuscany, Italy.

About 800 riders of all nationalities take part, many of them sporting 1940s bikes, woollen jerseys and leather saddles. Even support teams and officials ride around in vintage cars, so as not to break the nostalgic spell.

The one-day race is run over four distances, from 75km to the epic 200km, much of which is run on *strade-bianchi* ('white roads') of wheel-stopping gravel. The participants are of varying levels of experience and skill, but all have one thing in common: a love affair with vintage cycling.

ARMSTRONG'S ACCOLADES

Lance Armstrong's domination of road racing and his well-documented battle with cancer brought him the kind of international recognition usually reserved for movie stars. In addition to his many racing trophies, which included a record seven Tour de France victories, Armstrong was showered with so many awards by media and sporting organisations that he himself must have lost track of his accolades. As a reminder, they included:

- Marca Legend Award [Spain] 2004
- Trophee de L'Academie des Sport [France] 2004
- BBC Sports Personality of the Year – Overseas Personality Award 2003
- Reuters Sportsman of the Year 2003
- Institute for International Sport – named as a Sports Ethics Fellow 2003
- Laureus World Sports Award for Sportsman of the Year 2003
- Associated Press Male Athlete of the Year (2002, 2003, 2004, 2005)
- Sports Illustrated – Sportsman of the Year 2002
- International Amateur Athletic Association Trophy 2000
- Prince of Asturias Award – sports category [Spain] 2000
- William Hill Sports Book of the Year (for *It's Not About the Bike: My Journey Back to Life*) 2000
- US Olympic Committee – Sportsman of the Year 1999, 2001, 2002, 2003
- Velo d'Or Award [France] 1999, 2000, 2001, 2003, 2004
- Premio Coppi-Bici d'Oro Trophy [Italy] 1999, 2000
- Mendrisio d'Oro Award [Switzerland] 1999

THE 100 CLUB: CYCLING CLUBS MORE THAN A CENTURY OLD

Shaftesbury Cycling Club (Mountnessing, Essex) was founded in Stratford, east London, in 1887, but its base moved eastward in line with the migration from city to suburb of many of its present-day members. The club is named in honour of philanthropist and politician Lord Shaftesbury (seventh Earl), who supported the club and owned the hall in which its early meetings were held.

Main activities: time trialling, road racing, long-distance touring

Club colours: red/black/gold

A BIKELY STORY

Bikely is a massively popular website (www.bikely.com) that allows cyclists to share route information. Since its launch in 2006, details have been posted on more than 12,000 routes around the world – including 1,000 in the UK.

Founder Jules Szemere, an Australian cyclist, intended Bikely for commuting cyclists to share safe, back-street routes through towns and cities, but the idea has also been taken up by long-distance tourers. Routes range from the challenging (the route of the first stage of the 2007 Tour de France, for example) to mountain bike classics like the Skyline trail at Afan Forest, Cardiff, Wales.

Routes can be viewed and printed from any computer with an internet connection. For more hi-tech riders, there is an option to download a file of your chosen route onto a global positioning system (GPS) mapping device. It's also easy to upload info onto the site, thus sharing your favourite bike rides with the world.

CROWD TROUBLE

In 1999, a spectator fired a can of pepper-spray into the peloton near the finish of stage 17, causing several riders to drop out. US team member Frankie Andreu wrote in his diary after the event: 'The amount of people watching the race every day is incredible. There are rows and rows of people lining the course. Some are nice, some are freaks, some are fans of cyclists – and maybe some are not.'

UK 100-MILE DISTANCE CYCLING RECORDS

Bicycle	Year	Rider(s)	Hrs/mins/secs
Men Single	1993	IS Cammish	3 11 11
Women Single	1991	PJ Strong	3 49 42
Men Tandem	1990	M Winter & S Winter	3 20 48
Women Tandem	1955	CM Watts & DR Grist	3 57 11
Mixed Tandem	1992	M Gray & Miss SE Wright	3 30 23

Tricycle	Year	Rider(s)	Hrs/mins/secs
Men Single	1991	DJ Pitt	3 39 51
Women Single	1971	J Noad	4 50 39
Men Tandem	1991	DJ Pitt & P Stonebanks	3 44 07
Mixed Tandem	1991	DJ Pitt & Ms L Lamont	3 36 47

32 *Year in 1900s when Charles Mochet designed the Velocar, a recumbent bicycle on which Francois Faure broke both the mile and kilometre records*

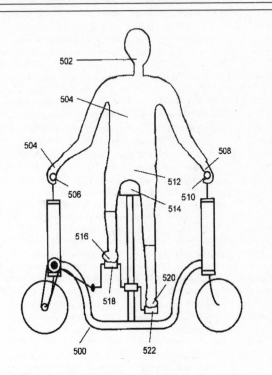

The sideways bicycle

A device that has to be seen to be believed, and one that turns 150 years of bicycle development on its head. Or rather, on its side. The sideways bike has steerable wheels with a set of handlebars at either end. The cyclist sits on a unicycle seat, at 90 degrees to the frame, and operates a wheel with each hand. Pedalling makes the bike travel sideways. The inventor claims that the front-to-back balance required to ride the bike affords 'tremendous grace and motion', adding: 'It's dance-like. The advantages are in the motion. It's never going to win you the Tour de France. But it's mesmerising and entertaining.'

Inventor: Michael Killian (Ireland)
Patent number: US2005029771, published February 2005

RIDING RIDDLES

Guess the bicycle-related solution to this puzzle
Religious service points out your failings as a road-user.

Answer on page 151.

CAPITAL CYCLING

**The most popular places to ride in London, according
to a survey of the capital's cyclists**

Along the River Thames or the canals: 17%
Richmond Park: 12%
Hyde Park: 7%
Epping Forest: 7%
Regents Park, Primrose Hill: 6%
Embankment: 4%
Hampstead Heath, Parliament Hill: 3%
Lea Valley: 3%

(Transport for London, 2003)

A BICYCLE THIEF TRAPPED

Cycle theft is not, by any means, a new problem. Even in Victorian times, riders struggled to keep light-fingered criminals from pinching their penny farthings.

And since relations between police and cyclists at the time were strained to say the least, it is somewhat surprising to learn of the lengths that one enterprising officer went to capture a serial offender, a youth named George Thomlinson.

According to a report from the cycling press in 1870, he had called at the house of Mr George Young, in Islington, north London, to try a bicycle that Mr Young had advertised for sale. 'He liked the machine so well that he tried it round the street corner, and it ran away with him, or he ran away with it; anyway, they both went off together, although not previously acquainted.'

Detective Henderson caught the rogue by placing a similar advertisement of a machine for sale at Kingsland. Mr Thomlinson called, as he had done in Mr Young's case, to try it. 'Unfortunately the bicycle was not at home, but Detective Henderson was, and he invited the inquirer to accompany him to the place where the machine was kept. Off they went, and walked together till Stoke Newington police station was reached...'

CYCLING COLLISIONS: A CRASH COURSE

Taking out insurance is not compulsory for cyclists, but for regular commuters it is an option well worth considering. Many cycling organisations, including the UK's national cyclists' organisation, CTC, provide personal injury cover and legal advice to members. In the event of an accident with another vehicle, there are several steps a cyclist should follow in order to increase their chance of making a successful claim:

1. Never admit that it was your fault.
2. Note the driver's name, address, vehicle registration number and insurance details.
3. Take names, telephone numbers and addresses of at least two witnesses.
4. Report the accident to the police.
5. If injured ensure that you seek medical advice from a hospital or your GP, and photograph your wounds.
6. Keep any damaged clothing and bike parts and try to obtain a written assessment of the damaged items.
7. If you incur any expenses as a direct result of the accident, make sure you keep a full record of these along with receipts where appropriate.
8. If you are insured, contact the company or organisation to help deal with a claim – whether it's one you are making, or one that's being made against you.

QUOTE UNQUOTE

A bicycle is a vehicle for revolution.
Daniel Behrman, author, *The Man Who Loved Bicycles*

FEELING FLAT – THE DEATH OF A TENOR

Louis Cazette had more reason than most cyclists to curse flat tyres. A famed French tenor singer of the early 1900s, he was widely tipped as being on the cusp of greatness when, at the age of 35, his life was cut suddenly short by a bizarre bicycling accident.

He died, it was said, from blood-poisoning after he cut his finger while mending a bicycle puncture. At least that was the official cause of death given at the time – later reports suggest this might have been invented to cover up the fact that he was fatally wounded in a rehearsal of the duel scene in Gounod's opera, *Mireille*.

CYCLE USE DOWN, BIKE LUST UP

According to a long-term study known as the National Transport Survey, bicycle use in the UK has been falling steadily since 1975 both in terms of the distance travelled and the number of trips. Yet the same study has shown that 42% of households in Britain owned at least one bicycle in 2001, compared with just 36% in 1991. The simple conclusion to be drawn is that, for some, the act of buying a bike rather than getting on it is as far as that virtuous New Year's resolution goes…

GHOST MACHINES

Mysterious, riderless white bicycles have been sighted in several big US cities over the last few years – including New York, Seattle and Chicago – stirring much intrigue and debate among residents and in the media. But these appearances have nothing to do with the paranormal. The bikes are chained to street furniture close to spots where cyclists have been killed or injured as 'eerie visual reminders', in the words of one newspaper report, of the dangers faced by riders.

A SPECTATOR'S GUIDE TO CYCLE SPORT

BMX

BMX stands for bicycle motocross – as the name suggests, the sport grew out of the popularity of its motorcycle equivalent. Since its birth in the 1960s, BMX has spread rapidly from the streets and dirt tracks of California to become a major international sport; there are now 75 national federations with official BMX activities recognised by the Union Cycliste Internationale, and the International Olympic Committee has decided to introduce BMX in the 2008 Olympic Games in Beijing.

Races are held on snaking, dirt-track circuits with jumps, banked corners and other obstacles adding to the excitement. Eight riders compete in each heat (qualifying rounds, quarter finals, semi-finals, finals), with the top four qualifying for the next round.

The other main competitive form of BMX is generally referred to as 'freestyle'. Pioneered in the 1970s and closely related to skateboarding – adherents of both sports can often be found sharing ramps and jumps in skate-parks – it is a predominantly urban art whose best practitioners put together stunning, gravity-defying sequences of tricks.

With lifted feet, hands still,
I am poised, and down the hill
Dart, with heedful mind;
The air goes by in a wind.

Swifter and yet more swift,
Till the heart with a mighty lift
Makes the lungs laugh, the throat cry:
'O bird, see; see, bird, I fly.

'Is this, is this your joy?
O bird, then I, though a boy
For a golden moment share
Your feathery life in air!'

Say, heart, is there aught like this
In a world that is full of bliss?
'Tis more than skating, bound
Steel-shod to the level ground.

Speed slackens now, I float
Awhile in my airy boat;
Till, when the wheels scarce crawl,
My feet to the treadles fall.

Alas, that the longest hill
Must end in a vale; but still,
Who climbs with toil, wheresoe'er,
Shall find wings waiting there.

Going down Hill on a Bicycle, A Boy's Song
by Henry Charles Beeching (1859-1919)

CYCLE COUTURE

Hermès

Only the most modish of cyclists would consider purchasing a bike produced by the French fashion house – to buy one would require a visit to their Sloane Street store in London. One recent model was covered in pale-green, hand-stitched Taurillon Clemence leather, and retailed for upwards of £1,000. In an earlier experiment, industrial designer Antoine Fritsch was commissioned by the company to produce a 'natural' bicycle with bamboo frame, cork handlebar grips and wooden wheel rims.

BLINK AND YOU'LL LOSE IT

A bicycle is stolen every 71 seconds in England, according to a study published in 2007.

Crime figures compiled by Halifax Insurance showed that 439,000 bikes, worth a total of £146 million, were stolen in a 12-month period between 2005-06, a 10% increase on the previous year. Almost 90% of thefts occurred when a cycle was left locked in public. Only 1% were stolen from an owner's home.

QUOTE UNQUOTE

It's not about the bike. It's a metaphor for life, not only the longest race in the world but also the most exalting and heartbreaking and potentially tragic.
Lance Armstrong, cyclist, on the Tour de France in
It's Not About the Bike: My Journey Back to Life

THE HOLY TRAIL – A GUIDE FOR PEDALLING PILGRIMS

Biking the pilgrim's way to Santiago

For centuries, Christian pilgrims have been following the Camino de Santiago ('Way of St James') through north-west Spain on foot and horseback. More recently, an increasing number have been using their bicycles to complete the historic journey to the Cathedral of Santiago de Compostela in Galicia – in 2000, one fifth of the 55,000 pilgrims were estimated to have cycled.

The cathedral authorities in Santiago require that pilgrims must carry the *credencial* ('pilgrim's passport'), and ensure it is stamped at each *refugio* ('stopover'). A pilgrimage can start anywhere, at any time, but cyclists must cycle the last 200km. A variety of routes can be taken, but the tunnel route (Irún to Santo Domingo de la Calzada) has the advantage of passing through the Basque Province of Guipuzcoa, which is also home to the Nuestra Señora de Dorleta (Sanctuary of Our Lady of Dorleta), a chapel-cum-cycling museum dedicated to Spain's patron saint of wheelmen.

Cyclists are warned that, whichever way you go, you are likely to encounter some very rough terrain and will need a sturdy bike as well as good physical fitness. The cathedral authorities suggest riders 'should train on a regular basis and get used to some new elements that would be part of the route... for example, by pedalling on narrow paths or up steeps with the saddlebags full'.

ANNUAL BICYCLE SALES IN THE UK

Based on sales reported to the Bicycle Association by its members, around 30 of the biggest distributors and manufacturers of bicycles in the country. The figures below are described as 'best estimates' by the Bicycle Association, for the simple reason that its members are rivals, and don't want to reveal their exact sales figures to one another.

1967	590,000 *(no BMX, no mountain bikes, pre-oil crisis)*
1970	600,000
1975	1.1m *(post-oil crisis)*
1980	1.6m
1984	2m *(peak of the 1980s BMX boom)*
1985	1.5m
1986	1.56m
1988	2.2m *(mountain bike boom)*
1989	2.5m
1990	2.2m
1991	2.2m
1992	2.2m
1993	2.25m
1994	2.35m
1995	2.15m
1996	2.44m
1997	2.52m
1998	2.32m
1999	2.38m
2000	2.3m
2001	2.5m
2003	2.5m
2004	4.5m

WRITERS ON BICYCLES

And as you rode along in the warm, keen air you had a sensation that the world was standing still and life would last for ever. Although you were pedalling with such energy you had a delicious feeling of laziness. You were quite happy when no one spoke, and if one of the party from sheer high spirits suddenly put on speed and shot ahead it was a joke that everyone laughed at and for a few minutes you pedalled as hard as you could.

W Somerset Maugham, *Cakes and Ale*, 1930

Year in 1900s when Tommy Godwin cycled 75,065 miles, averaging 39
205.66 miles a day, to set the world mileage endurance record for cycling

DAISY BELL

This song, composed by Harry Dacre in 1892, is better known by its refrain ('Daisy, Daisy!') than its title.

The story behind the lyrics, according to David Ewen, writing in *American Popular Songs*, goes like this: 'When Dacre, an English popular composer, first came to the United States, he brought with him a bicycle, for which he was charged duty. His friend (the songwriter William Jerome) remarked lightly: "It's lucky you didn't bring a bicycle built for two, otherwise you'd have to pay double duty." Dacre was so taken with the phrase "bicycle built for two" that he decided to use it in a song.'

The resulting ditty gained success in London, where it became something of a standard for music hall star Kate Lawrence, and in New York where it was sung to great acclaim by Jennie Lindsay.

It is said that the real-life Daisy who inspired the song was the Countess of Warwick, Frances Evelyn Maynard, one of the wealthiest and most desirable English women of the age. A pioneering socialist, campaigner for women's rights and Labour parliamentary candidate, not to mention mistress of the Prince of Wales, 'Daisy' eventually married John Boyd Dunlop, founder of the Dunlop rubber company and inventor of the pneumatic tyre – which would ensure all future tandem-riding couples a smoother ride.

There is a flower within my heart,
Daisy, Daisy!
Planted one day by a glancing dart,
Planted by Daisy Bell!
Whether she loves me or loves me not,
Sometimes it's hard to tell;
Yet I am longing to share the lot
Of beautiful Daisy Bell!

Chorus:
Daisy Daisy,
Give me your answer do!
I'm half crazy,
All for the love of you!
It won't be a stylish marriage,
I can't afford a carriage,
But you'll look sweet upon the seat
Of a bicycle built for two!

Number of schools involved in the 2007 trial stage of Bike It, a scheme funded by the UK cycle industry to encourage pupils to start cycling

We will go 'tandem' as man and wife,
Daisy, Daisy!
Ped'ling away down the road of life,
I and my Daisy Bell!
When the road's dark we can despise
P'liceman and lamps as well;
There are bright lights in the dazzling eyes
Of beautiful Daisy Bell!

Chorus

I will stand by you in 'wheel' or woe,
Daisy, Daisy!
You'll be the bell(e) which I'll ring, you know!
Sweet little Daisy Bell!
You'll take the lead in each trip we take,
Then if I don't do well;
I will permit you to use the brake,
My beautiful Daisy Bell!

Melody and lyrics by Harry Dacre, 1892

OLD PICTURE, NEW CAPTION

*Myrtle warned Bert for the last time to keep his pinkies
on the handlebars and out of her bloomers.*

CHECK YOURSELF BEFORE
YOU WRECK YOURSELF

It pays to take extra precautions when riding off-road, and these words of advice from Natural England could save you from discomfort, stress and even injury:

• Check local weather reports before heading for the hills – don't take the weather for granted as bad weather can descend very quickly.

• Invest in a first-aid kit and know how to use it.

• Carry emergency rations. A high-carbohydrate energy bar lasts for years.

• Take a map and a compass and know how to use them.

• Carry essential tools such as a bike pump and a spare inner tube.

• If you are caught in low-visibility conditions, stop until the weather clears and find shelter. Put on spare dry clothing and sit on something dry. If you are cold, keep your limbs moving. Stay awake and huddle close to companions.

• Tell somebody where you are going and report any changes of plan by telephone.

• Plan the route. Make sure it is within the capabilities of the weakest member of your group. Allow enough time to return well before nightfall.

• Avoid going solo if possible. Three is the minimum safe number. In an accident, one can go for help; the other stays with the injured.

• Wear the right clothes (include reflective gear) and footwear. Take spare clothing.

WRITERS ON BICYCLES

The journey back was even more eerie than the journey out, the moon now behind them, their shadows before, and as they climbed the hills the mountains climbed before them as if to bar their way and when they rushed downward to the leaden bowl that was the lake, and into the closed gulley of the coom, it was as if they were cycling not through space but through a maw of Time that would never move.

Sean O'Faolain,
'Silence of the Valley' from
The Man Who Invented Sin, 1948

RACING THROUGH THE PAGES

Ten best-selling books about cycle racing

1. *It's Not About the Bike: My Journey Back to Life*, by Lance Armstrong
2. *The Death of Marco Pantani: A Biography*, by Matt Rendell
3. *The Hour*, by Michael Hutchinson
4. *Every Second Counts*, by Lance Armstrong
5. *In Search of Robert Millar: Unravelling the Mystery Surrounding Britain's Most Successful Tour de France Cyclist*, by Richard Moore
6. *A Century of Cycling: The Classic Races and Legendary Champions*, by Sean Kelly and William Fotheringham
7. *The Escape Artist: Life from the Saddle*, by Matt Seaton
8. *The Beautiful Machine: A Life in Cycling, from Tour de France to Cinder Hill* by Graeme Fife
9. *Bad Blood: The Secret Life of the Tour de France*, by Jeremy Whittle
10. *Rough Ride*, by Paul Kimmage

QUOTE UNQUOTE

Get a bicycle. You will not regret it, if you live.
Mark Twain, writer, in his article 'Taming the Bicycle'

SILENT WITNESS

On 17 May every year, cyclists all over the world take part in mass rides that share one peculiar feature: they are carried out in complete silence.

There is no talking, singing, or ringing of bells; nothing but the sound of rolling tyres and clicking gears as scores of riders take to the roads in memory of cyclists who have been killed by motor vehicles in their cities.

The first Ride of Silence took place in Dallas, Texas, in 2003, after endurance cyclist Larry Schwartz was hit by the mirror of a passing bus and was killed. In the UK, silent rides are organised in London, Aberdeen and Yeovil, while overseas events are run as far afield as Chile and Cyprus.

All participants are asked to wear black armbands, and to refrain from carrying banners or other protest materials. As the organisers say, 'the power of the event is in the silence of the participants'.

ALL-TIME TOP 25 ROAD RACERS

Cycling Hall of Fame, an authoritative website dedicated to cycle sport, analyses results from 17 major events on the racing calendar to compare the achievements of riders from different eras. Its list of the 25 best riders of all time (as at May 2007) was as follows:

1. Eddy Merckx, BEL
2. Bernard Hinault, FRA
3. Fausto Coppi, ITA
4. Jacques Anquetil, FRA,
5. Gino Bartali, ITA
6. Lance Armstrong, US
7. Miguel Indurain, ESP
8. Felice Gimondi, ITA
9. Joop Zoetemelk, HOL
10. Louison Bobet, FRA
11. Greg Lemond, US
12. Raymond Poulidor, FRA
13. Francesco Moser, ITA
14. Rik Van Looy, BEL
15. Alfredo Binda, ITA
16. Sean Kelly, IRE
17. Lucien Van Impe, BEL
18. Jan Ullrich, GER
19. Erik Zabel, GER
20. Federico Bahamontes, ESP
21. Laurent Fignon, FRA
22. Jan Janssen, HOL
23. Charly Gaul, LUX
24. Gustave Garrigou, FRA
25. Roger De Vlaeminck, BEL

THE IRON MAN

The Saab Salomon Mountain Mayhem, which claims to be the world's largest 24-hour mountain biking 'festival', is a tough UK endurance race that's known for attracting gluttons for off-road punishment.

But in 2005, post-race reports gave special mention to Paul Roberts, a mountain biker and 'extreme ironing' aficionado who completed the solo event with an ironing board and iron strapped to his back – managing a not unrespectable 44th place despite his extra load. It is not known how many shirts he managed to press during the event.

44 *Age of Finnish rider Teuvo Louhivuori when he broke the 24-hour endurance record in 1974, cycling 830.1km in a day*

THE 100 CLUB: CYCLING CLUBS MORE THAN A CENTURY OLD

Cambridge University Cycling Club, founded in 1874. Besides racing, the club is also the umbrella organisation for recreational cycling in Cambridge, one of England's most cycle-centric places.

Main activities: road racing, mountain biking, leisure touring.

Famous members: Gerard Francis Cobb (1838-1904) writer and composer, was club president as well as the first president of the National Cyclists' Union; Ion Grant Neville Keith-Falconer (1856-1887), Arabic scholar and champion amateur cyclist who, in June 1882, became the first recorded end-to-end wheeler, pedalling from Land's End to John O' Groat's in just under 13 days.

RIDING RIDDLES

Who is this famous cyclist?
A GLANCE, MRS TORN
Answer on page 151.

Answer on page 151.

PRIZED POSSESSIONS

As well as booty and prestige, the winners of professional road races often have to find space on their mantelpieces for some singular trophies, including the following prizes:

The Paris-Roubaix cobblestone – A plinth bearing a giant cobblestone, just like the ones the riders ride over for long stretches of the one-day classic nicknamed 'the hell of the north'. Holding the great slab of rock aloft on the podium after competing in such a gruelling event is a feat in itself.

The San Sebastian 'Txapela' – The traditional, floppy black hat of Spain's Basque region, in which the race is held. Probably the one piece of headgear that looks more daft than a cycle helmet.

The Kuurne-Brussels-Kuurne stuffed donkey – Surely the most sought-after cuddly toy in any professional sport. The donkey is the symbol of Kuurne and the nickname for local people in the town, apparently renowned throughout Belgium for their stubbornness.

Cost per mile in thousands of pounds to build the 45
National Cycle Network

WRITERS ON BICYCLES

Lady Brandon, out for a ride on her 'strong, powerful' bay horse, stops to tell a passing cyclist why his two-wheeler can never be as useful as a real steed...

'That's all bosh,' said Lady Brandon impetuously. 'It stumbles, and gives you the most awful tosses, and it goes lame by its treadles and thingamejigs coming off, and it wears out, and is twice as much trouble to keep clean and scrape the mud off as a horse, and all sorts of things. I think the most ridiculous sight in the world is a man on a bicycle, working away with his feet as hard as he possibly can, and believing that his horse is carrying him instead of, as anyone can see, he carrying the horse. You needn't tell me that it isn't easier to walk in the ordinary way than to drag a great dead iron thing along with you. It's not good sense.'

George Bernard Shaw,
An Unsocial Socialist, 1887

STEP UP A GEAR – THE RISE OF SPORTIVES

If you feel that cycling a few miles to work every day is not the best use of your legs or your carbon-frame speed machine, and are looking to justify all those racing jerseys you've bought but never worn, 'cyclosportives' could be just the tonic.

These events, which appeal to every type of cycle enthusiast from the time-trialling clubman to the occasional trail rider, offer a taste of professional road racing without the all-out competitiveness. They are a great test of a rider's skill and fitness, with courses covering distances of 50-150 miles and often involving some tough climbs.

The thing to remember is that sportives are massed-start events, but not races – riders generally want to record the best possible time, but they are not competing against one another.

The UK scene has undergone rapid expansion in recent years, with new events popping up all over the country. There has been a particular surge in interest in sportives that are tied in with major professional races. For instance, all 5,000 places on the British Cyclosportive (covering the 120-mile London to Canterbury stage of the 2007 Tour de France) were sold within 24 hours.

To find details of sportive and other challenge events near you, visit the website www.cyclosport.co.uk.

SEX AND CYCLING

Ready to ride

Some cyclists believe sex should be avoided on the night ahead of a big race, for fear that it might somehow blunt their competitive edge, or drain their bodies of the energy needed to overcome rivals in a bunch sprint. Not so the hard-living, hard-racing, five times Tour de France winner Jacques Anquetil, who famously said: 'To prepare for a race there is nothing better than a good pheasant, some champagne and a woman.'

BEST BMX-ERS

The top five professional BMX riders, past and present, as chosen by Matt Hoffman (a veteran who would no doubt feature on most other riders' lists) for *UK Ride BMX* magazine:

1. Taj Mihelich
2. Colin Winkelman
3. Kevin Robinson
4. Seth Kimbrough
5. Anthony Napolitan

WHEEL HEALTHY

Cycling is close to being an ideal form of exercise for the following reasons:

• It is aerobic – it uses major muscle groups (in the legs) and causes the heart rate and respiration to increase in order to supply the muscles.

• It is low weight bearing – because the cycle takes the weight of the body off the legs, much less pressure is exerted on the joints than in running, for example. Cycling is therefore a good form of exercise for people with joint problems.

• Those who are deterred by other sports-related activities, may find cycling acceptable. It can take them out into the countryside, which has been shown to have health benefits.

• It is a low-skill activity. Although the prospect of cycling on Britain's roads may appear challenging to a non-cyclist, it is essentially a skill that is readily and quickly learnt, and once acquired, it's never forgotten.

OLD PICTURE, NEW CAPTION

Hugo looked down at the yellow-ish puddle forming around his shoes and realised that he had still not overcome his childish fear of thunder and lightening.

QUOTE UNQUOTE

After your first day of cycling one dream is inevitable. A memory of motion lingers in the muscles of your legs, and round and round they seem to go.
HG Wells, author, *The Wheels of Chance*

POPULAR LONG-DISTANCE CYCLE ROUTES IN ENGLAND

Land's End to John o'Groats

Cycling the length of mainland Britain from the toe of Cornwall through to the tip of Scotland is an ambition that many cyclists aspire to and thousands fulfil each year. Record holder Gethin Butler completed the 840-mile journey in 44 hours, four minutes and 19 seconds, but most take two weeks to enjoy CTC's 1,000-mile scenic (hilly!) route. This journey takes you through North Cornwall and Devon, up along the Welsh borders, through the Peak District and Pennines, the Borders, Grampians and Highlands.

DON'T CYCLE, BOOGIE!

Cycling has provided the inspiration for some of pop's strangest moments. Here is an iPod-ready compilation of the top 10 riding records spanning the last 40 years:

'Bicycle Race' by Queen (*Jazz*, 1978)
No one looked better in Lycra bib-tights than Freddie Mercury, particularly when he was belting out the unforgettable chorus of this paean to the joys of bicycling (some have suggested he was singing about bisexuality, but that's just ridiculous).

'Bike' by Pink Floyd (*The Piper at the Gates of Dawn*, 1967)
In which Syd Barrett attempts to impress a girl by showing off his handsome-looking machine. Lets himself down by admitting that the bike in question is not his.

'Nine Million Bicycles' by Katie Melua (*Piece by Piece*, 2005)
The number of bikes in Beijing. In 2007, Melua announced plans to raise money for Save the Children by cycling along the Great Wall of China.

'Riding on My Bike' by Madness (single, 1982)
London's nutty boys backed the 12-inch version of their hit single 'Driving in my Car' with this upbeat ode to green transport.

'Tour de France '03' by Kraftwerk (*Tour de France Soundtracks*, 2003)
After writing albums dedicated to motorways and railroads, the electro-pop pioneers turn their attention to the 'man-machine'.

'The Acoustic Motorbike' by Luka Bloom (*The Acoustic Motorbike*, 1992)
The Irish folk singer's evocative account of pumping his thighs through the rural delights of Kerry on a Muddy Fox.

'Motorcrash' by The Sugarcubes (*Life's Too Good*, 1988)
Bjork sings of riding about on her bicycle, administering first aid to the victims of road accidents.

'The Pushbike Song' by The Mixtures (single, 1970)
Classic early 1970s pop record, charming or cheesy depending on your state of mind. Reached number two in the UK charts, and still a karaoke staple.

'My White Bicycle' by Tomorrow (*Tomorrow*, 1968)
Cult British psychedelic band sing of a utopian experiment by the Provos, an anarchist/situationist group in Amsterdam, who left white bicycles around the city for anyone to use.

'Happy Cycling' by Boards of Canada (*Peel Sessions* ep, 1999)
Spaced-out instrumental from the Scottish electronica duo that makes no reference to cycling bar the title, but could provide the perfect soundtrack to a gentle ride on a summer's day.

A GOOD TURN

Charity bike rides allow you to indulge in your favourite hobby while raising money for worthy causes – what's not to like? Here are some of the biggest and best of the annual events:

Royal National Lifeboats Institute: The Tour de Tendring (May)

The RNLI tour of rural Essex has become established as one of the most successful charity cycle rides in the country, and celebrated its 15th year in 2007. Riders have a choice of three routes of varying lengths, all of which start and finish on Dovercourt Seafront, and take in some picturesque villages and scenery.

British Heart Foundation: The London to Brighton Bike Ride (June)

Since it started in 1980, the 54-mile ride has raised more than £35m for the BHF and has attracted around 700,000 participants. Even though there are 27,000 places available each year, the event is always over-subscribed, and priority is given to applications of riders who raised at least £100 in the previous year. The charity also organises several other annual rides, including London to Southend (58 miles) and Oxford to Cambridge (85 miles).

Action Medical Research: The London to Paris Bike Ride (July)

One of the more challenging of the charity rides, which requires its 700 riders to cover 300 miles in four days. The payoff for all that hard work? Participants get to ride along the Champs-Élysées, one day before the start of the Tour de France, and then stay on to soak up the atmosphere of the race. The ride raises funds to support the charity's Touching Tiny Lives campaign, which aims to give the most vulnerable babies a better start in life.

CTC: Phil and Friends Challenge (August)

Now firmly established as the UK's match for the Etape du Tour, this is one of three annual rides that raise funds for the CTC Charitable Trust. The 150km and 100km routes pass through some of the Peak District's most beautiful scenery and toughest terrain, including Winnats Pass and Holme Moss.

Marie Curie Cancer Care: The South Down Bike Ride (September)

This ride, first held in 1995, offers a choice of three routes of varying lengths and takes in the beautiful countryside in the Castle Ward, Strangford and Downpatrick areas of Northern Ireland.

BIKE vs HORSE

In a little-reported, seven-mile race between 'two French bicyclists and a fast horse', held in St Germain, near Paris, on 6 October 1878, the results were as follows:

Charles Terront (bicyclist): *20 minutes and 2 seconds*
The horse (rider unknown): *20 minutes and 28 seconds*
M Grossin (bicyclist): *21 minutes*

It is possible the horse had no inkling of the victor's pedigree: Monsieur Terront was already winning bicycle races all over France, and in the coming years he would become known far and wide as one of the fastest men on two wheels. His career highlights – other than coming first in the horse race, of course – include winning the first Paris-Brest-Paris race in 1891.

PEDALLING PLACENAMES

Ten UK locations made for cycling:
Chain Hill, Stapleford, Salisbury
Crank Road, Crank, St Helens, Merseyside
Cycle Road, Nottingham
Cycle Street, York
Saddle Rise, Chelmsford, Essex
Velos Walk, Cambridge
Wheelabout Wood, Lincolnshire
Wheel Burn, Scottish Borders
Wheeler Way, Shanklin, Isle of Wight
Wheely Down, Hampshire

QUOTE UNQUOTE

Bicycles are quiet and slight, difficult for normal motorised humans to see and hear. People pull out in front of bicycles, open car doors in their path, and drive through intersections filled with the things. The insubstantial bicycle and its unshielded rider are defenceless against these actions. It's a simple matter of natural selection. The bicycle will be extinct within the decade. And what a relief that will be.
PJ O'Rourke, author, *Republican Party Reptile*

WACKY RACERS:
WONDERFUL BICYCLE INVENTIONS

Hot rod

Bicycles are a good way of getting to your favourite remote fishing spot. Unfortunately, they are not the best vehicles when it comes to carrying rods; that's where this wonderful invention comes in. The simple addition of a fishing pole holder, comprising a series of wire hoops on a shaft, will make the journey easier and safer. And of course there's no reason why such a device couldn't be adapted to accommodate

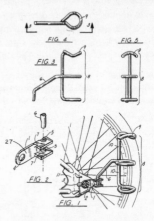

paraphernalia of other hobbies and sports; snooker cues and javelins spring instantly to mind. Watch out for speed bumps, though, or you might find yourself inadvertently launching missiles from your back wheel.

Inventor: Grady M Engolia (US)

Patent number: US6273391, filed August 2001

ONE-WHEELED EPIC

On 13 April 1999, Kurt Osburn set off on a coast-to-coast bike journey from Hollywood, California, to Orlando, Florida. He completed the 2,839.6-mile ride on 25 June – a not inconsiderable feat, especially considering he chose to use just one of his two perfectly good wheels.

Osburn – also known as 'the wheelie king' – set a Guinness World Record and become the first person in history to ride a bicycle wheelie coast to coast. According to the official account of his feat, he averaged 50 miles a day with winds in excess of 40mph, travelled on the 110 Highway, was chased by dogs almost every day, suffered four flat tyres, and made more than 1.8 million pedal revolutions from start to finish.

'I never knew America was such a big country. You just don't realise how far it is coast to coast,' he said afterwards.

WHY CYCLING IS GOOD FOR YOU

A series of recent studies have shown the enormous health benefits of riding a bicycle:

• A population-wide study in Copenhagen found that, compared with those who cycled regularly to work, people who did not do so had a 39% higher mortality rate, regardless of whether or not they cycled or took part in other physical activities at other times.

• Regular cyclists typically enjoy a level of fitness equivalent to someone 10 years younger, and those cycling regularly beyond their mid-30s could add two years to their life expectancy.

• Whitehall civil servants who cycled for at least an hour a week (or 25 miles in a single week) had less than half the death rate of those who didn't, during a nine-year study period.

• Another UK study found that people who took up cycling as a new activity gained the greatest benefits at the outset, but fitness continued to improve as they increased their cycle use. Reduced body fat was also noted, particularly among those who were overweight or obese at the outset of the trial.

RIDING RIDDLES

Who is this famous cyclist?
A PANIC AT MORN
Answer on page 151.

FILL THAT HOLE

All road cyclists know the elbow-rattling judder that comes with riding over a pothole. But they are more than just a nuisance, they are a danger to both rider and bike.

The problem, according to the the UK's national cyclists' organisation, CTC, is widespread: 12% of compensation claims made by its members relate to injuries caused by potholes and road defects.

But there is something you can do: by visiting fillthathole.org.uk, an interactive reporting-site set up by CTC, riders can pinpoint potholes using Google maps. The information will then be passed on to the relevant local authority, which has a duty to repair the road.

EARLY CYCLING DITTIES

The Hill Climber

Let others sing the praises of a country that is flat,
The good hill-climbing bicyclist will never relish that,
But when he's out upon his wheel his course will always tend
To where the meadows undulate, and roads are set on end.

Let others hymn the glories of a scorch around a track
Where croppers on the cinders ornament them blue and black,
Give me the wild ferocious joy to muscularly cope
Against the force of gravity upon a rutty slope.

Let others tell of level roads, monotonous and straight,
O'er which they treadle easily at quite a rapid rate,
I love a bit of collar-work, and dearly like to ride
Up every danger-boarded hill, and coast the other side.

I've climbed the hill at Westerham, upon a sixty-inch,
At Muswell or at Reigate I was never known to flinch;
And when I've weathered Weatheroak, and knocked off Knockaroon,
I mean to go and ride up all the mountains in the Moon.

From *Duffersville – Its Cycling Chronicles and
Other Sketches*, AJ Wilson (ed), 1889

CYCLE COUTURE

Rolling down the catwalk

The first fashion show dedicated to cycle style took place in London in June 2007. *Prêt à Rouler* (French for 'ready to roll') featured bike-riding models sporting what the organisers billed as 'dream cycle clothing'.

The idea behind the show, launched by hip London bike store Velorution, and backed by Transport for London, was to showcase designer solutions to the problem of what to wear on a bike – particularly for urban commuters who need something that works both in and out of the saddle, for work and social engagements.

Featured labels included Vexed Generation, which worked with sportswear giant Puma to design the 'biomega' folding urban bike and a line of 'urban mobility' clothing (key piece: a leather zip-up cyclist's hoodie); Third Transition, which uses organic cotton and water-based inks; and Junky Styling, which specialises in recycling cast-off clothes as designer garments.

PIMP MY RIDE C.1896

Custom paint jobs are not a recent fad – even in the early days of cycling, aristocrats found ways of making their steeds stand out from the crowd.

'It is certainly the exception nowadays to see a bicycle with ordinary black or unembellished paint,' wrote Mrs F Harcourt Williams in *The Complete Cyclist* in 1896. 'Most women and many men have their machines painted in their own particular colours. Lady Huntingdon, for instance, has her machine painted green with primrose lines upon it; Miss Cornwallis West's colours are crimson and blue; Princess Henry of Plesse has the prettiest white machine that ever was seen; and no expense was spared in the finishing off of General Stracey's machine, which is done in the well-known red and blue of the Guards.'

THE VALUE OF CYCLING

The annual retail value of cycles sold in the UK:

1988	£250m
1989	£310m
1990	£305m
1991	£297m
1992	£311m
1993	£300m
1994	£300m
1995	£350m
1996	£375m
1997	£420m
1998	£365m
1999	£426m

QUEEN'S NAKED RACE

When rock band Queen rented Wimbledon Stadium for a day in 1978 to shoot the video for their double A-side single 'Bicycle Race'/'Fat Bottomed Girls', a considerable quantity of naked models were hired to stage a nude bicycle race.

Afterwards, according to a version of the tale related in *Rock 'n' Roll London* by Max Wooldridge, bicycle suppliers Halfords refused to take the saddles back, knowing what they'd been used for.

If the same thing happened today, any salesperson would undoubtedly have no problem with the used saddles – they could make a small fortune selling them on eBay...

Typical diameter in inches of the front wheel of an 'ordinary' bicycle 55 or 'penny farthing'

We should not be surprised, in these times of increasing eco-awareness, at the way politicians harness bike power whenever they feel the need to boost their green credentials.

A short while after coming to power in 1997, Tony Blair cut a youthful figure as he cycled with fellow European leaders through the streets of Amsterdam at the start of his first EU summit. Here was the image of a modern continental leader, one who would have cyclists in mind when shaping policy. Early signs were promising – the Labour government's 10-year transport plan envisaged a trebling of annual cycle journeys by 2010. By the time Mr Blair stepped down in 2007, however, that aspiration appeared to have been quietly forgotten.

David Cameron started cycling to Westminster soon after he became Tory leader in 2006. The MP looked like the real thing – white trainers, red waterproof jacket, black helmet – and media coverage helpfully tied his eco-friendly commute to a Conservative local election campaign focused on the environment ('Vote Blue, Go Green'). It soon emerged that his bicycle rides to the House of Commons had been followed by an official car, carrying his suitcase and shoes.

The 2004 US presidential race took an unlikely diversion when both the main candidates – President George Bush and Democrat challenger John Kerry – started clocking up miles (and column inches) on their bikes. The US media began comparing styles: Kerry, the veteran cyclist who favours a $6,000 Serotta road bike and long-distance rides, versus the president, a recent convert to cycling who enjoyed pootling about on his mountain bike, a similarly-priced Trek Fuel 98 (aka 'Mountain Bike One').

The New York Times referred to it as a clash between road-riding 'wussies' and MTB-favouring 'sensation seekers'. Both men crashed their bikes in front of reporters during the campaign: Kerry skidded on sand in the road during a Sunday ride near Boston, and Bush flew over the handlebars on an off-road path after uttering the immortal words: 'I'm gonna show you a hill that would choke a mule'.

Both men got straight back on the bike – or at least the campaign trail, despite heavy ridicule in the media over their pratfalls – and the US-voting public decided the sensation seeker should win the race.

56 *Number of cycle 'vibration-damping', or suspension, devices exhibited at the Stanley Show in 1890*

WACKY RACERS:
WONDERFUL BICYCLE INVENTIONS

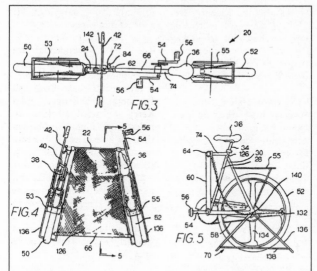

Restful ride

Ever get halfway there and decide you're just too tired to go on? The chair-bike is designed for the most laid-back of riders, allowing them to stop and take in their surroundings in comfort whenever the desire arises. The front and rear wheels of the bicycle fold out 'to form a substantially U-shaped frame onto which a seat fabric may be stretched to form a sling chair'. The fabric can be stowed in a roller tube and 'deployed in a manner similar to that of a retractable window shade'. Retractable stands under the wheels provide the chair legs.

Inventor: Ruowei Strange (US)

Patent number: US6688627, filed February 2004

QUOTE UNQUOTE

I hope that cycling in London will become almost
Chinese in its ubiquity.
Boris Johnson, MP, *The Guardian*

HOW GREEN IS MY JOURNEY?

Comparison of various modes of transport, from an ecological point of view, with a private car for an identical journey with the same number of people and over the same distance.

Base = 100 (private car without catalytic converter)

A: Car; B: Car with catalytic converter; C: bus; D: bicycle
E: aeroplane; F: train

	A	B	C	D	E	F
Space consumption	100	100	10	8	1	6
Primary energy consumption	100	100	30	0	405	34
CO_2	100	100	29	0	420	30
Nitrogen oxides	100	15	9	0	290	4
Hydrocarbons	100	15	8	0	140	2
CO	100	15	2	0	93	1
Total atmospheric pollution	100	15	9	0	250	3
Risk of accidents	100	100	9	2	12	3

Source: UPI Report, Heidelberg, 1989,
quoted by European Commission

RUSSIA'S RIDING REVOLUTION

What have bikes and The Beatles got in common? Both have been banned in Russia – bicycles were prohibited under Czarism, while the mop-tops were kept at bay by the Iron Curtain.

In the late 1800s, as cycling was gaining swathes of devotees across England and France, Imperial Russia remained impervious to the charms of the sport, at least in St Petersburg.

In 1893, however, there was a sudden and unexpected thaw in relations, reported with some glee in the English press. 'Those who are conversant with the conditions under which cycling is practised in the land of the Czar will be aware that for many a long day riding in St Petersburg has been absolutely forbidden,' ran one report. 'Owing, however, chiefly to the instrumentality of General Vladimirovitch Struckhoff – the Chief Engineer attached to the Police Master General von Wahl's Chancery, and a sportsman of the first water – the prohibition has been withdrawn, and the prospects of the pastime have been materially improved.'

The article goes on to list many conditions for riding on the streets, among them that riders have to be over 18 and must take a test to show they can ride a 'figure of eight' between two points within a prescribed radius.

BICYCLE BISTROS

Places for riders to refuel on both sides of the Atlantic:

The Bicycle Club
Type of food: Traditional American
Signature dish: BBQ chicken and half-rack ribs
Location: 487 Sylvan Avenue, Englewood Cliffs, New Jersey, US

The Bicycle
Type of food: Global fusion
Signature dish: Sashimi tuna and avocado tartare
Location: 1444 Light Street, Baltimore, Maryland, US

Ye Olde Bicycle Café
Type of food: Snacks and coffee
Signature dish: Fruit smoothie

Location: 6792 University Avenue, San Diego, California, US

Bombay Bicycle Club
Type of food: Indian
Signature dish: Tandoori mixed grill
Location: Restaurants and delivery service across London, UK

The Blue Bicycle Restaurant
Type of food: Seafood
Signature dish: Baked monkfish wrapped in Parma ham with fondant potato, black olive tapenade and red pesto dressing
Location: 34 Fossgate, York, UK

QUOTE UNQUOTE

Bikes talk to each other like dogs, they wag their wheels and tinkle their bells, the riders let their mounts mingle.
Daniel Behrman, author, *The Man Who Loved Bicycles*

KEEP YOUR HANDS ON YOUR BARS...

...or you might end up behind some. In 2006, a bicycle courier in Colombia ended up in court after he grabbed a woman pedestrian's bottom.

According to local news reports, the courier had cycled off after groping her, but had been caught by passers-by. When the courier was arrested, the victim was given the option of slapping him, letting him go or filing a complaint – she decided to take him to court in an effort to set a precedent that would stop sexist behaviour.

The judge ruled that the messenger had committed an abusive sexual act and sentenced him to four years in jail.

Percentage of parents of children that cycled to school regularly who noticed 59 improvements in their physical development (2007 Cycling England survey)

Scotland is not known chiefly for its cuisine, but in 2006 Spokes, a cycling campaign group based in the Lothians, ran a competition among its members to find the best recipes for bonk-beating food*.

The judges picked the winners according to five criteria: transportability (is your food easy to carry on a bike ride?), healthiness (not too much saturated fat), cooking skills and preparation time required, cost and food miles (how many non-UK ingredients).

The top entry was the 'Sustrans Scotland Super-Snack', submitted by Sustrans Scotland Staff, which consisted simply of a cheese and tomato roll with a piece of fruit and chocolate.

More interesting, however, was the runner-up, 'Snack Attack Brack', by Christine Thompson, reprinted here for hungry cyclists to try:

Preparation time: Overnight soak plus 10 minutes
Cooking time: 1.5 to 2 hours

Ingredients:
One cup of tea (without milk)
450g mixed dried fruit
1 cup brown sugar
2 cups self-raising flour
1 well-beaten egg

Instructions:
1. Overnight: soak fruit and sugar in tea
2. Next day: Pre-heat oven to gas mark 3/150°C
3. Mix all ingredients together
4. Pour into well greased 21x11x5cm loaf tin
5. Bake for 1.5 to 2 hours, or until knife comes out clean

Its creator advises: 'Easy to make, transport and keep (in a tin)... Full of energy, but without added fat... Smells fantastic when cooking... Try spreading with extra energy – butter, margarine, honey or jam – or eat it plain.'

* *'The bonk' is the name given to the sudden and debilitating state a rider enters after spending too long in the saddle without food.*

RIDING RIDDLES

Guess the bicycle-related solution to this puzzle
Ensuring a smooth ride to an ancient Phoenician city.

Answer on page 151.

*Dorothy vowed to never again to make curry for
her husband the night before a tandem ride.*

THE HOLY TRAIL – A GUIDE FOR
PEDALLING PILGRIMS

Cyclists' Memorial Service at Meriden, Warwickshire

The Green in the West Midlands village of Meriden – known as the geographical heart of England – has been a place of pilgrimage for cyclists for more than 85 years.

Ever since 21 May 1921, when a monument dedicated to cyclists killed in World War I was unveiled in Meriden, riders from every corner of the country have converged on the village for an annual memorial service.

The original unveiling of the monument (a 6m-high obelisk) was attended by 20,000 cyclists, many of whom laid wreaths, and the ceremony was carried out by Lord Birkenhead (who was Lord Chancellor at the time). In 1963, a bronze plaque was added to the shaft of the obelisk to commemorate cyclists who died during World War II.

In recent years, numbers attending the Cyclists' Memorial Service have fallen to the low hundreds, but it remains one of the largest gatherings of cyclists – and the most poignant.

Diameter in centimetres of CTC's cast-iron 'winged wheel' signs, placed 61 on hotels and other buildings to mark a cyclist-friendly stopping place

WRITERS ON BICYCLES

A clash of philosophies

The writer George Bernard Shaw was among the many young men who were swept up by the cycling craze in the late 19th century, and by all accounts he was one of the most fanatical and reckless of riders. One biographer, Olivia Coolidge, noted that 'over and over again he risked his life by putting up his feet in the days before free-wheelers and tearing down hill around blind corners as though possessed'. No doubt this led to many spills and near-misses, including the following head-on collision with the philosopher Bertrand Russell in or around 1896:

'At this time he [GBS] and I were involved in a bicycle accident, which I feared for a moment might have bought his career to a premature close. He was only just learning to ride a bicycle, and he ran into my machine with such force that he was hurled through the air and landed on his back 20 feet from the place of the collision. However, he got up completely unhurt and continued his ride; whereas my bicycle was smashed, and I had to return by train. It was a very slow train, and at every station Shaw with his bicycle appeared on the platform, put his head into the carriage and jeered. I suspect that he regarded the whole incident as proof of the virtues of vegetarianism.'

Bertrand Russell, *Portraits from Memory and Other Essays,* **1956**

BICYCLE KICKS

The most spectacular way of scoring a goal in football is, undoubtedly, with a move known as a bicycle kick (aka scissors, or overhead, kick).

It is also among the most difficult and athletic things you can do with a ball, although being a cyclist should give you a slight advantage over the general population in that you are already reasonably fit and mobile, and you know how to move your legs in a pedalling motion. The challenge, of course, lies in applying this technique in a slightly different way: you only have to pedal through one revolution, on an imaginary bike, and you have to do so while throwing yourself head over heels through the air.

Timing is also of the essence – missing the ball entirely and landing on your face will make you look rather silly, so make sure you get it right before you try it in a game with friends.

Percentage of cycling-related deaths involving head injury, according to a 1995 US study

FROM LAND'S END TO JOHN O'GROATS

The official UK record holders for this ride from one end of Great Britain to the other

Bicycle	Year	Rider(s)	Days/hrs/mins/secs
Men Single	2001	G Butler	1 20 04 19
Women Single	2002	LEA Taylor	2 04 45 11
Men Tandem	1966	PM Swinden & WJ Withers	2 02 14 25
Mixed Tandem	2000	A Wilkinson & Miss LEA Taylor	2 03 19 23

Tricycle	Year	Rider(s)	Days/hrs/mins/secs
Men Single	1992	R Dadswell	2 05 29 01
Men Tandem	1954	A Crimes & JF Arnold	2 04 26 00

US AND THEM

An international comparison of bicycle use as a proportion of all commuter journeys

US: 0.4%

Canada: 1.2%

UK: 2%

Japan: 9%

Germany: 11%

Switzerland: 15%

Denmark: 18%

Netherlands: 27%

A SPECTATOR'S GUIDE TO CYCLE SPORT

Cycle ball

Yes, football on wheels, played by two teams of two players (who act both as goalkeepers and outfield players). A match is made up of two seven-minute halves. The ball (approximately 18cm in diameter), which can be struck with either the front or the rear wheel, is filled with horsehair and can reach a speed of 37mph. Inside the penalty area, the goalkeeper can use his hands to stop shots on goal. The goal measures 2 x 2m. As in football, fouls are penalised by free kicks and penalties. The most successful exponents of the sport were the Pospísil brothers, from the former Czechoslovakia, who won 20 World Championships between 1965 and 1988.

CYCLING ORGANISATIONS IN THE UK

CTC

The UK's biggest and oldest national cycling membership organisation, founded in 1878 as the Bicycle Touring Club. Today the CTC has a 70,000-strong membership and services include a cyclists' helpline, access to local groups, third-party insurance and legal aid.
www.ctc.org.uk

British Cycling

British Cycling is the internationally recognised governing body of cycling in the UK. It covers road racing, track cycling, cyclo-cross, BMX, mountain biking, cycle speedway and, in Scotland, road time trials. The organisation's duties include selecting the Great Britain teams for the Olympics.
www.britishcycling.org.uk

Sustrans

Charity promoting sustainable transport, primarily through the creation of the National Cycle Network. In the last decade, Sustrans has seen the completion of 10,000 miles of safe cycle routes throughout the country.
www.sustrans.org.uk

Rough Stuff Fellowship

Formed in 1955 – long before the US-led boom in mountain biking – by British cyclists dedicated to off-road riding.
www.rsf.org.uk

The Tandem Club

Formed in 1971, primarily to provide otherwise unobtainable spare parts and technical advice on how to maintain older machines. Since then, the club has extended the range of services to include organised rides and events and support for riders with disabilities.
www.tandem-club.org.uk

Audax UK

The foremost long-distance cycling association in the UK. Oversees the running of long-distance cycling events and validates and records every successful ride.
www.aukweb.net/index.htm

Road Records Association

Ratifies times and distances for 20 different records, including 12- and 24-hour rides, 100- and 1,000-mile rides, and some famous point-to-point rides such as Land's End to John O'Groats.
www.rra.org.uk

Cycling Time Trials

Originally formed as the Road Racing Council in 1922 and becoming known as Cycling Time Trials in 2002, CTT ensures uniformity in the conduct of road time trials, with around 1,000 clubs as members.
www.cyclingtimetrials.org.uk

London Cycling Campaign

LCC is a charity that lobbies for improved facilities and aims to raise the profile of cycling across the capital. Members receive benefits such as insurance deals and discounts in selected shops.
www.lcc.org.uk

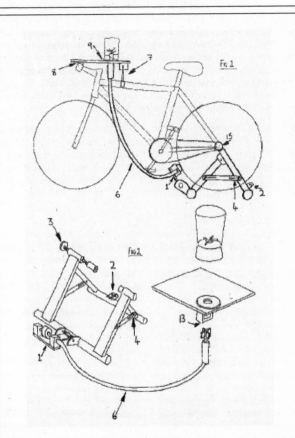

Food for thought

There can surely be no better way of beating 'the bonk' than using your bicycle to prepare food as you ride. This arrangement for 'generating and supplying rotational energy' from a bicycle wheel to a food blender is the perfect solution for the hungry cyclist.

Inventor: Thomas Briggs (Great Britain)

Patent number: GB2404641, filed February 2005

Number of naked models hired by Queen in 1978 to stage a nude bike race for the video of their single 'Bicycle Race'/'Fat Bottomed Girls' 65

THE 100 CLUB: CYCLING CLUBS MORE THAN A CENTURY OLD

CTC: The UK's national cyclists' organisation was founded in 1878 as the Bicycle Touring Club and renamed the Cyclists' Touring Club in 1883. CTC's campaigning voice went to work instantly establishing cycles as 'carriages' in 1888 with the right to use the roads, getting the right to cycle on bridleways incorporated in the 1968 Countryside Act, changing Scottish law giving cyclists a right in law to cycle freely off-road in 2005 and in 2007 successfully changing the highway code to benefit cyclists.

Benefits of membership include: A huge collection of information on routes now available to members via the internet, a cyclists' helpline offering advice on all cycling matters, an entire department dedicated to campaigning on behalf of cyclists' rights, local groups, a wide range of rides and events, £5 million third-party insurance and free legal advice, and discounts on accommodation, accessories and travel.

THE CATCHER OF THE FLY

The health benefits of cycling are well-documented, but not many people know of the bicycle's use as a tool for research into tropical disease.

Frank L Lambrecht, a medical scientist who worked for the Red Cross in Congo in the late 1940s, was engaged in an important study of the tsetse fly (which transmits the parasitic disease known as 'sleeping sickness' to humans) when he struck upon a novel way of monitoring how the insects spread from place to place.

To test his theory that the tsetse was often introduced to new areas by human and cattle movement, he had one of his 'fly-boys' ride a bicycle from his camp in Kindama to the Akanyaru swamps (along the Rwanda-Burundi border). According to Lambrecht's memoirs, a screen covered in an unspecified 'sticky substance' was fitted to the machine in order to capture insects along the route.

The rider made 74 runs inside the 'flybelt' (the area where the tsetse was present), each for 2,500m, and the number of flies caught was recorded every 500m. The tally was 538. Lambrecht's fly-catching cyclist was then called on for another 74 sprints, this time of 5,500m, through a tsetse-free corridor. This time 75 flies were caught. The conclusion? That 'flies were present outside the main flybelt, most probably those that had followed the bicycle'.

LESSER KNOWN HEROES OF CYCLING

Stanley Cotterell (born in 1857) surrendered his prospects as a medical student in order to become the founder, first secretary, newsletter editor and later president of CTC. In his time he saw it grow into an organisation known throughout the world, with cycle touring established as the most popular of all outdoor recreations.

Thomas 'Biddy' Bidlake (1867-1933) was a prolific figure within cycle racing. He broke over 100 road and path records and his tricycle record of 410 miles 1,110 yards over 24 hours stood for over 40 years. The Bidlake Memorial Prize – for the most outstanding performance or contribution to cycling – has been won by Tom Simpson, Graeme Obree and Nicole Cooke, among others.

George Stancer (1878-1962) was perhaps the UK's most formidable cycling advocate, one of its greatest writers and the father of modern cycle campaigning. When the Ministry of Transport was set up in 1919 Stancer was one of the first to lobby for cyclists' representation on its committees and had huge influence on numerous acts.

Eileen Gray OBE was in 1946 part of the first group of women to ride for Great Britain. The next year she lobbied successfully for girls to compete for their own National Titles on the track and eventually went on to become president of the British Cycling Federation.

Beryl Burton OBE (1937-1996) was an English racing cyclist winning more than 90 UK championships and seven world titles throughout her career. In 1967 (21 years before women's cycling became part of the Olympics) she set a new 12-hour time trial record of 277.25 miles – a distance that for two years remained unbeaten by man or woman.

The development of cycling over the last 130 years has relied almost entirely on the work of people behind the scenes; people who for the most part received little or no remuneration or recognition. Of particular note are the thousands of unsung heroes of cycling – those who didn't win any races, but behind the scenes made as great a contribution as their more visible sporting counterparts. Hats off to them.

QUOTE UNQUOTE

A bicycle ride is a flight from sadness.
James E Starr, author, *The Literary Cyclist*

ALSO KNOWN AS

Nicknames for famous road races

Tour de France – *Grand boucle*, French for 'big loop'.

Tour de Lombardy – 'Race of the falling leaves', because it takes place at the beginning of October.

Paris-Nice – 'Race to the sun', because it leaves Paris for the south of France in early March.

Paris-Roubaix – *L'enfer du Nord*, French for 'hell of the north', because of the treacherous terrain and conditions.

Milan-San Remo – *La Primavera*, from the Italian for 'spring', the season in which the race is held.

Tirreno-Adriatico – 'Race of the two seas', because it follows a route between the Tyrrhenian and Adriatic coasts of Italy.

Liège-Bastogne-Liège – *La Doyenne*, loosely translated from the French for 'mature woman', because this is the oldest of the five 'monuments' (one-day classics) of European cycle racing.

QUOTE UNQUOTE

The bike is a stroke of genius. On that day in the 19th century when Michaux put a chain and pedals on it, it had practically attained its final form. Since then they've refined the details, they've been fanatical about the subtleties, but the basics of the machine are the same.
Paul Fournel, author, *Need for the Bike*

WRITERS ON BICYCLES

The sight of a broken-down machine is to the overhauler as a wayside corpse to a crow; he swoops down upon it with a friendly yell of triumph. At first I used to try politeness, I would say: 'It is nothing; don't you trouble. You ride on, and enjoy yourself, I beg it of you as a favour; please go away.' Experience has taught me, however, that courtesy is of no use in such an extremity. Now I say: 'You go away and leave the thing alone, or I will knock your head off.' And if you look determined, and have a good stout cudgel in your hand, you can generally drive him off.

Jerome K Jerome,
Three Men on the Bummel, 1900

The edition of the Giro d'Italia at which, in 1985, Bernard Hinault won and became the only cyclist to have won each Grand Tour more than once

THE LONGEST BICYCLE

The longest bicycle as defined by the *Guinness World Records* book (two wheels and no stabilisers), was 28.1m long and built by members of Gezelschap Leeghwater, the mechanical engineering students' association at Delft University of Technology. It was ridden for more than 100m at Delft, The Netherlands on 11 December 2002. This broke the previous record set by the Super Tandem Club Ceparana, of Italy, whose long-runner (25.9m) was ridden by 40 members of the club on 20 September 1998.

WHY CYCLISTS WON'T STOP

Everyone likes to keep moving, but cyclists have more reason than most for conserving their momentum. According to an article written by Chris Juden, the technical officer for the UK's national cyclists' organisation, CTC, riding a bike at a steady speed takes only about as much energy as to walk at one quarter that speed.

Cycling at 12mph equates to 3mph walking. Each requires about 75 watts of power from the 'human engine' and people are as happy to cycle four miles to work as they are to walk one mile. Each should take from 20 minutes up to half an hour, including stops, at a total energy expenditure of some 100 kJ.

Every time a cyclist or pedestrian stops, they lose kinetic energy and have to work harder upon starting off in order to accelerate and restore that energy. It is interesting to see just how far a cyclist could go, at a given speed, for the same amount of energy as may be required to reach that speed.

This gives a direct measure of the energy cost of stopping.

For typical cycling speeds, of 10-12mph, on a middling kind of bicycle, it can be calculated that one stop-start is equivalent to cycling an additional 100m. Compare this with the pedestrian, who can stop and start again with no more energy than it takes to make a couple of steps.

This explains why cyclists, if riding on a cycle path following a footway, are extremely disinclined to give way at side roads. Compared to a pedestrian, doing so adds considerable extra time to their journey.

Of course, a cyclist's journey is likely to be four times as long as a pedestrian's, so any given stop doesn't add such a big percentage to it; but by the same token, this means the cyclist may cross four times as many side roads in the course of such a journey. It also explains why cyclists sometimes find it easier to take a longer route without so many junctions.

FENDING OFF FIDO

If you ride regularly, you are likely at some point to meet an angry, unrestrained dog. The following tips should help you pedal away unscathed:

Understand the dog
The most common reason for a dog to give chase is that it wants to defend its territory from what it thinks is a fast-moving intruder – or it wants to play. Once you are well past its home turf, the dog will lose interest.

If things turn nasty, stay calm and assert your authority
On rare occasions, a dog might launch an all-out attack rather than give you a friendly warning. You should be able to identify the animal's intent by how hard it is running and its expression: a full-out sprint with ears back, tail down and bared teeth could mean trouble. For anything less than a definite charge, try ignoring the dog in the hope that it will eventually turn back. If it gets too close, shout 'No!' or 'Go home!' in as confident a manner as you can muster.

Pedal hard
Dogs often approach from the rear. Even one sitting up ahead will wait until you pass before attacking. You can use this to your advantage by suddenly accelerating just before reaching the dog – then just keep going until you are out of range.

Protect your front wheel
Sometimes, a feisty dog might occasionally try to ambush you by running out in front of your bike – avoid hitting it with your front wheel as this will almost certainly send you flying.

Make some noise – or a splash
There are lots of anti-dog weapons on the market for cyclists (including pepper sprays and ammonia), but if you want to avoid such extreme measures, you can use your water bottle to spray an aggressive mutt; ringing your bell could also cause enough of a distraction for you to make a getaway.

Last man standing
Should all of the above fail, get off and walk the bike, keeping it between you and the dog as a shield. If you carry a pump, it can help keep a snapping dog at a distance and, as a last resort, you can use your bike as a weapon.

QUOTE UNQUOTE

It's a sport of self-abuse.
Lance Armstrong, cyclist,
It's Not About the Bike: My Journey Back to Life

OLD PICTURE, NEW CAPTION

*Timothy, an inveterate tinkerer, finally threw in the
towel and agreed to call a bike mechanic.*

RIDING RIDDLES

A cyclist wanted to keep an appointment at 5pm. If he started at
noon and rode at 15mph he would arrive there one hour too soon,
while if he started at the same time and rode at 10mph he would
get there an hour too late. How far had he to ride?

Answer on page 151.

EXTREME CYCLING

Cycling in outer space

In 2000, the space shuttle *Atlantis* made a special journey to the
International Space Station... to drop off an exercise bike. The
stationary cycle was placed over a large porthole window in the floor,
allowing exercising astronauts to ride with the world at their feet,
literally. Crew member Ed Lu described the experience in his journal:
'I ride the bike four times a week, and do a variety of workouts from
intervals with bursts at high resistance, to longer workouts at lower
resistance. The riding motion is a little different than what you might
have in a gym on the ground since you don't actually sit on a seat...
If you ride the bike for 90 minutes, you can ride all the way around
the world – so Lance Armstrong eat your heart out!'

THE HIGH LIFE

CTC's *Cycle* magazine's must-do top 10 high rides:

Rosedale Chimney, North York Moors (OS Grid reference: SE 724 958) – This 1 in 3 climb is the pinnacle as the steepest road in Britain.

Hardknott and Wrynose, The Lake District (OS Grid reference: NY 313 034) – These two hills joined together claim to be the toughest in Britain and regularly burns out car clutches.

Winnats Pass, The Peak District (OS Grid reference: SK140 828) – Dead straight and with a howling head wind, this climb, cut through steep sided rock offers no respite.

Holme Moss, The Peak District (OS Grid reference: SE 108 059) – The northern classic at 3 miles long just goes on and on...

The Long Mynd, Shropshire (OS Grid reference: SO 456 936) – Used as the national hill climb course- won by Olympic champion Chris Boardman.

Bealach Na Ba, Scottish Highlands (OS Grid reference: NG 711 445) – Not excessively steep, just exposed and hard, but with arguably the best view over to Skye.

Corrieyairack Pas, Scottish Highlands (OS Grid reference: NH 379 090) – Don't be afraid to push on this 7 mile off-road rutted and rocky epic.

Bwlch Y Groes, North Wales (OS Grid reference: SH 858 149) – Stunning scenery rewards after the 1 in 5 climb over the highest road pass in Wales.

The Devil's Staircase, Mid Wales (OS Grid reference: SN 854 527) – Pace yourself as this roller coaster climb just keeps on getting steeper.

The Wayfarer, North Wales (OS Grid reference: SJ 057 410) – Feel like a mountaineer on this hard slog up this wild and open off-road ride.

CYCLADELIC, MAN!

Albert Hofmann is the Swiss chemist who discovered the hallucinogenic drug LSD. He initially found out about its strange effects by accidentally ingesting a tiny amount. A few days later, on 19 April 1943, he decided to experiment by taking 25mg of the drug. Here is a brief excerpt from his chronicle of what happened on his ride home on what has since become known in scientific circles (and narcotic folklore) as Bicycle Day: 'It became clear that the symptoms were much stronger than the first time. I had great difficulty in speaking coherently, my field of vision swayed before me, and objects appeared distorted like the images in curved mirrors. I had the impression of being unable to move from the spot, although my assistant told me afterwards that we had cycled at a good pace.'

Percentage increase in the number of cycle journeys made on London's major roads since 2000

WRITERS ON BICYCLES

It is by riding a bicycle that you learn the contours of a country best, since you have to sweat up the hills and coast down them. Thus you remember them as they actually are, while in a motor car only a high hill impresses you, and you have no such accurate remembrance of country you have driven through as you gain by riding a bicycle.

Ernest Hemingway, *By-Line*, 1968

TEN CYCLING STORIES FOR CHILDREN

Mrs Armitage on Wheels, by Quentin Blake
Bear on a Bike, by Stella Blackstone
The Bike Lesson, by Stan and Jan Berenstain
The Big Bike Race, by Lucy Jane Bledsoe
Curious George Rides a Bike, by Hans Augusto Rey
The Bicycle Man, by Allen Say
Gracie Goat's Big Bike Race, by Erin Mirabella
Mike and the Bike, by Michael Ward (foreword by Lance Armstrong)
Topsy and Tim Ride Their Bikes, by Jean and Gareth Adamson
A Bike for Big-Ears (Make Way for Noddy), by Enid Blyton

SEX AND CYCLING

Wheel love

Most cyclists will admit to having a certain affection for their steeds; some even go so far as to think of them as good companions on life's journey. But how many would admit to falling head over heels in love with a bicycle? Irish writer Flann O'Brien must have seen a good few cases of such lust in his time, because he describes the phenomenon in detail in the novel *The Third Policeman* (written 1940, published posthumously 1967). In one scene, when the protagonist prepares to escape from a police cell on the arresting officer's cycle, we see what one critic referred to as 'quite lavish and sexually symbolic praise' of the two-wheeled love object. Here's a brief excerpt from the passage in question: 'How desirable her seat was, how charming the invitation of her slim encircling handle-arms, how unaccountably competent and reassuring her pump resting warmly against her rear thigh!'

CELLULOID CYCLISTS

Top 10 films featuring two-wheelers, as chosen by Andy Salkeld, organiser of the Leicester Bike Film Festival.

1. *Bicycle Thieves*, 1948. Oscar-winning masterpiece of Italian neo-realism in which Antonio goes in search of his stolen bike.

2. *Red Light Go*, 2002. A tight-knit group of US bike messengers compete in dangerous 'alley cat' races on busy city streets.

3. *The Cyclist*, 1987. Moving tale of an Afghan refugee in Iran who is offered a chance to make some money by riding a bicycle continuously for seven days and nights in a circus ring.

4. *Le Tour de France – The Official History, 1903-2003*, 2003. Celebrates a century of the premier cycling event from the first race in 1903, won by Maurice Garin, to Lance Armstrong's fifth consecutive victory in 2003.

5. *The Brit Pack*, 2003. Homage to British cyclists who have taken part in the Tour de France, including Robert Millar, Chris Boardman and Sean Yates.

6. *Belleville Rendez-Vous*, 2003. Animated adventure of a young, would-be champion who is kidnapped by cycling villains.

7. *O Caminho das Nuvens* ('The Road to the Clouds'), 2003. The true tale of an unemployed truck driver who undertakes an epic cycle journey from the north-east of Brazil to Rio de Janeiro in search of work.

8. *To Russia with Love*, 2004. Following a group of British BMX riders and skateboarders on a road trip to Moscow, where they plan to ride around Red Square.

9. *Pee-wee's Big Adventure*, 1985. Tim Burton's technicolour remake of *Bicycle Thieves*.

10. *Jour de Fête*, 1949. Heart-warming comedy of French rural life, following the cycling postman (Jacques Tati), who is inspired to speed up his rounds after watching a documentary about super-efficient couriers in the US.

RIDING RIDDLES

Who is this famous cyclist?
AGILE MUD IN RUIN

Answer on page 151.

CYCLE COUTURE

Paul Smith

In keeping with the trend for designer versions of everything from scooters to mobile phones, British designer Paul Smith has joined forces with bespoke cycle makers Mercian to create some rather fine-looking – and predictably costly – bikes. The designer, who rode a Mercian as a youngster and 'fell into fashion' aged 17 after a cycling accident put an end to his hopes of becoming a professional racing cyclist, has worked on limited edition touring and track models with the Derby-based firm. The track bike is available in six classic colour combinations including 'blue/maroon frame, purple lugs and barber's pole, finished with yellow lining', while the touring model comes in 'tones of yellow/orange/mustard or blue/purple/turquoise'. These additions to the autumn/winter collection are hand-built with quality Campagnolo components and weigh in at just under £3,000 apiece. Perfect for the catwalk, one would imagine, but probably not ideal for the daily commute.

SAFETY IN NUMBERS

Sustrans, the sustainable transport charity, carried out a study of international statistics that suggest that as the proportion of cyclists in the population increases, the risk of accident lessens.

Percent of journeys by bicycle:
UK 2.3%, Denmark 18%, Netherlands 27%
Casualties per 100 million kilometres travelled:
UK 8, Denmark 1, Netherlands 0.8

However, other factors must also be considered. For example, Denmark and the Netherlands are two of the European countries with the highest provision of dedicated cycle lanes.

WRITERS ON BICYCLES

As I rode my bike, music began to happen to me. Insofar as I am able to describe it it was orchestral music. The piano was often involved, but on the whole the music was that of a large orchestra which had become a single instrument.

William Saroyan, *The Bicycle Rider in Beverly Hills,* 1952

The world record for the longest distance travelled in one hour is one of the most prestigious prizes in cycling, and has been contested by some of the sport's leading figures, including multiple Tour winners Jacques Anquetil and Eddy Merckx.

The earliest record was set in 1876 by an Englishman, FL Dodds, who achieved 26.508km on a penny farthing at Cambridge University Ground. But the first official 'hour', as recognised by the Union Cycliste Internationale (UCI), was set in Paris in 1893 by Henri Desgrange (who would go on to found the Tour de France): he covered 35.325km. The 40km barrier was broken in 1898 by American rider Willie Hamilton, who set a distance of 40.781km in Denver, Colorado.

The first great head-to-head contest involved French rider Marcel Berthet and Oscar Egg of Switzerland, who between them set six consecutive records between 1907 and 1914. Egg's 1914 record of 44.247km lasted almost 20 years.

At the other end of the 20th century, a similarly intense rivalry developed between two British riders, Graham Obree and Chris Boardman, who made use of technologically advanced bikes and the revolutionary 'superman' riding position. Obree held the record (51.596km) for one week in July 1993 before it was taken by Boardman (52.270km); Obree re-claimed it the following year with a ride of 52.713km. After brief spells in the hands of Miguel Indurain and Tony Rominger, in 1996 Boardman took the record for the third time with a distance of 56.375km.

However, in September 2000, the UCI announced that in order to limit the effect of technology and ensure that 'human effort' remained the principle factor, strict rules about equipment would be imposed on the official record. Essentially, this restricted competitors to traditional upright bikes and banning the use of time trial helmets, 'aero' bars, and disc wheels. The rules were applied retrospectively – all the way back to Eddy Merckx's 1972 record of 49.431km. This meant that Boardman's 1996 record was effectively downgraded, to a new sub-category of 'Best Hour Performance' (which Boardman still holds).

He responded one month after the UCI decision by setting a new UCI 'best hour' record on a traditional bike – bettering Merckx by just 10m. His distance of 49.441km lasted five years; it was broken in 2005 by Ondrej Sosenka, of the Czech Republic. His record of 49.7km remains unbeaten (at time of publication).

OLD PICTURE, NEW CAPTION

Between Cardington and Church Stretton
SHROPSHIRE.

That tree in the distance seemed to keep getting further and
further away from Linda and Tom... maybe there was
something in those biscuits they had for lunch.

A SPECTATOR'S GUIDE TO CYCLE SPORT

Cyclo-cross

Cyclo-cross is a cross-country event that combines cycling with
running; some of the terrain is so steep or muddy as to be unrideable,
so riders dismount and 'hike their bike' over their shoulder. Its origins
can be traced back to the tough winter training regimes of early road
racers; the first world championships were held in 1950. It is
traditionally an autumn and winter sport, with massed starts and
relatively short races over a distance of about 1.5 miles, usually lasting
no longer than one hour. Cyclo-Cross bikes look very similar to road
machines, but are adapted for bumpier terrain with stronger frames,
knobbly tyres, lower gears and a more upright riding position. Unlike
mountain bike racers, 'cross' competitors are allowed to use technical
support teams – in the event of a crash, they can continue the race on
a replacement bike rather than having to carry out makeshift repairs.

RIDE WITH THE DEVIL

One racing fan is as familiar to the sport's followers as even the most famous riders: the devil – aka Didi Senft – a German who has been following the race in his unmistakable red costume since the early 1990s.

The bearded Didi, or *Le Diable* as he is better known, has been a regular feature of all major cycling events including the Tour de France, the Giro d'Italia and the UCI Road World Championships.

His manic routine involves wearing red tights and horns, and chasing riders around various stages with his aluminium pitch fork in a bid to spur them on; not to mention posing for souvenir photographs with race fans. The stir he causes has not gone unnoticed: like everything else in the grand tours, the devil is now sponsored (by a German car parts firm).

Senft's commitment to cycling is not restricted to fancy dress, however. When out of costume, he is busy in his workshop knocking out 'fun' bikes – he has had at least 10 entries in the *Guinness World Records* book in recent years, including the world's largest and longest rideable bicycle: 7.8m long and 3.7m high.

WORDSMITHS AND WHEELERS

Ten great writers known to have a love of cycling

HG Wells
Leo Tolstoy
George Bernard Shaw
William Golding
Arthur Conan Doyle
Thomas Hardy
Ernest Hemingway
F Scott Fitzgerald
Alan Sillitoe
Vladimir Nabokov

CROWD TROUBLE

Lance Armstrong came a cropper in the 2003 Tour de France when his brake lever caught a spectator's 'musette' (bag containing energy snacks for competitors). Armstrong went head-first over his bars, and landed heavily on his left side. However, he managed to recover and went on to win the race.

PARKING SPACES

In cities, finding somewhere safe to store your bike is just as fraught a process as finding a car parking spot. Facilities such as those at the Finsbury Park Cycle Park in north London – the UK's largest automated, staffed cycle parking – could provide the answer.

It was built as part of a comprehensive upgrade at Finsbury Park station – one of the busiest tube, rail and bus termini in London – by Transport for London and opened in March 2006.

The sheltered park boasts 125 lockable bike racks with 24-hour access, operated by a smart card, and staffed at peak times.

SONG CYCLE

If you thought that tuning up a bicycle is something done only in a repair workshop, think again. Bikes are a favourite instrument among modern composers, and various cycle parts have been known to appear in the concert hall or recording studio alongside strings and woodwind.

Richard Lerman's 1979 'sound art' piece *Travelon Gamelon* is performed by attaching microphones to the wheels of bicycles in motion, and loudspeakers to the handlebars, thus amplifying the 'eerily beautiful internal sounds' reverberating through the frame. These are blended with sounds made by striking the spokes with metal or wood. Lerman produced a detailed score describing how to produce *Travelon Gamelon* in concert; one performance in Boston, US, involved more than 30 cyclists and musicians.

The Dudafoon is one of the many musical inventions of Godfried-Willem Raes, a leading avant-garde composer from Belgium. This electro-acoustic instrument-cum-sculpture is made of a bicycle wheel, springs and scrap metal, mounted on a wooden case that acts as a loudspeaker enclosure, modelled on Marcel Duchamp's dadaist work, *Roue de Bicyclette*. The sounds made by the spokes of the wheel as they are turned are amplified via a series of microphones.

Raes also composed *Symphony for Singing Bicycles*, as performed in London in July 2007 to coincide with the Prologue Time Trial of the Tour de France. The performance – essentially the amplified sounds of a group of cyclists riding around on various road surfaces – was organised by *The Bike Show* (a UK radio show broadcast on Resonance FM and via internet podcasts).

Number of days in which Nick Sanders cycled round the world in 1985 79
– breaking his own previous record of 138 days

WRITERS ON BICYCLES

I came out for exercise, gentle exercise, and to notice the scenery and to botanise. And no sooner do I get on that accursed machine than off I go hammer and tongs; I never look to right or left, never notice a flower, never see a view – get hot, juicy, red – like a grilled chop. Get me on that machine and I have to go.

HG Wells, *The Wheels of Chance*, 1896

QUOTE UNQUOTE

I like suburbs; nothing is ugly. Bicycling in the suburbs of a great city, I see a strange beauty in those quiet deserted evenings with the few remaining children showing off in the evening sunlight, laburnums and lilac weeping over the front gate, father smoking his pipe and rolling the lawn, mother knitting at the open window.
John Betjeman, former poet laureate

SMALL WHEELS GOOD

The original Moulton bicycle was launched late in 1962, and with its small (16-inch) wheels, dual suspension and open frame (no crossbar), marked one of the few successful attempts to challenge the traditional diamond-framed bicycle.

It dominated the 1962 Cycle Show at London's Earls Court, where it made its first public appearance, and went on to become a best-selling icon of the Swinging Sixties, favoured by pop stars and politicians as well as the general public.

But riders of larger machines should not be fooled into thinking that the Moulton is slow or unsturdy. In all its incarnations, from the original 1960s 'F frame' to the more recent 'AM' models, the Moulton has proved itself more than a match for conventional sports and touring cycles. Here are some of its most notable feats:

• One week after its launch, John Woodburn, riding a Moulton Speed, broke the Cardiff-London record by more than 18 minutes.

• In 1986, Jim Glover twice broke the flying 200m HPV record for the standard riding position in a fully streamlined AM.

• Dave Bogdan twice completed the single-stage Race Across America on an AM (1987 and 1988), his best time being 3,073 miles in just over 10 days and 15 hours.

Number of kilometres of cycle paths and walkways that developers plan to build to connect the areas surrounding London's 2012 Olympic sites

ULTIMATE BIKE BLING

In 2005, a bejewelled Trek Madone bicycle was sold at auction to raise money for the Lance Armstrong Foundation. The bike, adorned with gold and diamonds, sold for $75,000 (around £40,000), making it the world's most expensive bicycle.

The main feature is a 'Diamond 7' plaque created by designer jeweller Alan Friedman and fixed to the front of the bicycle. The plaque, fashioned from white and yellow gold, contains seven one-carat diamonds, each coloured yellow (like the winner's jersey) to represent Armstrong's Tour de France victories.

The bike was bought by an anonymous donor, presumably someone wealthy enough to own their own race track or a very large driveway, since one would think them unlikely to be taking it for a spin on public roads.

HOLLYWOOD WHEELERS

Ten screen stars who've been spotted in the saddle by treehugger.com's Hollywood Bike Patrol

George Clooney
Hilary Duff
Tom Hanks
Daryl Hannah
Matthew Modine
Arnold Schwarzenegger
Chloe Sevigny
Keifer Sutherland
Naomi Watts
Robin Williams

KINGS OF THE HILL

The products, places and people that made the most impact on trail-riding in 2006, as voted for by the readers of *Singletrack* mountain bike magazine (www.singletrackworld.com).

Best UK Trail Centre: Glentress, Scotland
Best Holiday Experience: Bike Verbier, Switzerland
Best Bike Shop: Sideways Cycles, Cheshire
Best UK Event: Fort William UCI Mountain Bike World Cup 2006
Best New Bike: Pace RC303
Mountain Bike Personality of the Year: Steve Peat, downhill rider

'RATIONALS' AND THE HAUTBOY AFFAIR

Just over a century ago, when cycling first achieved mass popularity, women cyclists began to enthuse over the benefits of 'rational' dress: variations on knickerbockers and a short coat in place of the customary long skirt and coat. The movement flourished, fostered by the new 'safety' bicycles (lower and easier to ride than penny farthings) and allied to other women's causes such as the Suffragette movement.

However, society at large was opposed to the idea of women wheelers, and took particular offence at those who dared to ride in their bloomers; there was a public outcry in 1893 when Tessie Reynolds, aged just 16 and dressed in rational attire, rode London-Brighton-London in eight and a half hours.

Critics of women cyclists included Eliza Linton, writing in *Lady's Realm* in 1896 that 'chief of all the dangers attending this new development of feminine freedom is the intoxication which comes with unfettered liberty'.

Cambridge undergraduates made a similar, though much cruder, point in 1897 by hanging a female student effigy – complete with bicycle – to protest the decision to include women's names on class lists.

The issue of rational dress came to a head two years later, when Lady Harberton arrived for lunch at the Hautboy Hotel at Ockham, Surrey, in 'rationals'. She was refused admission to the genteel coffee room and relegated to the public bar, not considered in those days at all the place for a woman. The CTC challenged the legality of the proprietor's actions and started proceedings. The club lost – but the wide reporting of the case is looked on as one of the opening shots in the campaign for women's rights.

BOOZE AND BIKES: A HEADY COMBINATION

Pub stops are, for many cyclists, an essential part of cycle tours in the countryside.

Beware how much you imbibe, however. Not only is it an offence to drink and ride, but cyclists are more likely to be killed or injured in a road traffic accident if they've been drinking alcohol, according to a US study.

The research, published in the *Journal of the American Medical Association* in 2001, indicates that drinking any amount up to the British legal limit (80mg of alcohol per 100ml of blood) could make a rider 20 times more likely to have a serious accident.

Amount of money in millions of pounds that UK riders spent on cycles and equipment at independent bicycle dealers in 2005

Many of the battles fought over 100 years ago will be more than a little familiar to cyclists today:

Then: In 1896, the 'rude way in which certain servants of the railway companies treat machines' prompted CTC to offer a prize of 20 guineas for the best design of a luggage van specially fitted for the safe conveyance of cycles.

Now: Following CTC's 'Keep cycling on track' campaign in 2007, which involved thousands of cyclists, the government announced a taskforce to represent cyclists during franchise agreements, as well as plans to promote cycle access and simplify cycle reservations.

Then: In 1939 a panel of experts from CTC devised the original Cycling Proficiency Test.

Now: In response to modern-day road conditions CTC suggested a new system of training for cyclists which was launched in 2006 as 'Bikeability'.

Then: The Road Traffic Act 1930 introduced the first Highway Code. Although motoring and pedestrian opinions were taken into account, cyclists were not consulted. Following petitions by CTC, amendments were accepted for the final draft.

Now: Following a high-profile campaign by CTC, the government agreed to amend over 40 rules in the Highway Code to the benefit of cyclists.

Then: In the 1880s several Norwich cyclists were injured when a cabman drove among them, injuring several, and was fined £6.

Now: CTC secured total compensation of £2.9 million between 2003-2007 on behalf of its members.

Then: Having lobbied for many years for all vehicles to carry a white light in front at night, CTC was successful in 1907 with the passing of the Lights on Vehicles Act.

Now: Following many years work by CTC, 2005 saw a liberalisation of cycle lighting law. Provided they are bright enough, flashers front and rear are now not only legal, but are all the lights you need.

AROUND THE WORLD ON A BICYCLE

A select list of long-distance cyclists and their memoirs

Thomas Stevens, *Around the World on a Bicycle* (1887)
The first trip around the globe on two wheels, in which Stevens covered an incredible 13,000 miles on a Columbia Expert high-wheeler, carrying little more than socks, a spare shirt, and a raincoat that doubled as a tent.

Thomas Gaskell Allen Jr and William Lewis Sachtleben, *Across Asia on a Bicycle* (1894)
Two student friends crossed Europe, Asia and America in the second circumnavigation of the world by bike. Their book covers the Asian leg of their journey (via the Gobi desert), which they describe as the 'longest continuous land journey ever made around the world'.

Sir John Foster Fraser, *Round the World on a Wheel* (1899)
The writer and two companions travelled through 17 countries on Humber one-speed bicycles, covering 19,287 miles in 774 days.

Louise J Sutherland, *I Follow the Wind* (1960)
Riding a one-speed bicycle with trailer attached, Sutherland became the first cyclist to follow the Amazon from source to sea.

Bernard Newman, *Speaking from Memory* (1960)
Prolific writer of travel books (and crime novels) who toured more than 60 countries over two decades.

Walter Stolle, *The World Beneath my Bicycle Wheels* (1978)
Setting off on what he thought would be a quick spin, he returned almost 20 years and 402,000 miles later.

Barbara Savage, *Miles from Nowhere* (1983)
Husband and wife team Larry and Barbara Savage tour 25 countries in two years, clocking up more than 20,000 miles (Barbara Savage died in a road traffic accident three years after completing the trip).

Ian Hibell and Clinton Trowbridge, *Into the Remote Places* (1985)
A record of several journeys. Hibell is one of the world's most famous cyclo-tourists, still pedalling away after more than 40 years on the road.

Josie Dew, *The Wind in My Wheels* (1992)
Four continents, 36 countries and 80,000 miles of cycling adventures are recorded in the first of Dew's highly popular travel memoirs.

WACKY RACERS:
WONDERFUL BICYCLE INVENTIONS

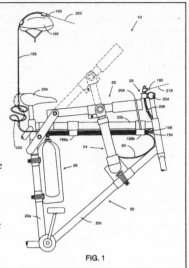

FIG. 1

High-pressure jet bike
Nothing's better than a water fight on a long hot day, but sometimes you need to bring in the heavy artillery to assert your superiority. It doesn't get much heavier than this, the aqua-assault weapon of choice: bicycle-mounted, pressurised water tanks and 'multiple trigger' systems connected to a series of 'high-velocity' jets – including one mounted on the rider's helmet. Potential uses abound: fending off aggressive dogs, squirting dangerous drivers, hosing down fellow cyclists on a hot hill climb...

Inventor: Michael Regalbuto (US)

Patent number: US5735440, filed April 1998

HIGHLAND HOSTEL

The first youth hostel in Britain is thought to have been a wooden hut at Ledard, Kinlochard, opened in the 1920s by the Rucksack Club – consisting of cyclists and hikers from Glasgow. To this day there is a hostel on the site of Ledard Farm, which offers accommodation in several 'bothies' and easy access to a network of forest cycling tracks and hill walks within Queen Elizabeth Forest Park.

WRITERS ON BICYCLES

When man invented the bicycle he reached the peak of his attainments. Here was a machine of precision and balance for the convenience of man. And (unlike subsequent inventions for man's convenience) the more he used it, the fitter his body became. Here, for once, was a product of man's brain that was entirely beneficial to those who used it, and of no harm or irritation to others. Progress should have stopped when man invented the bicycle.

Elizabeth West, *Hovel in the Hills*, 1977

BROADCASTERS ON BIKES

Jeremy Paxman *(presenter, BBC2's* Newsnight*)*

Jon Snow *(presenter,* Channel 4 News*)*

Sophie Raworth *(presenter, BBC1's* One O'Clock News*)*

Desmond Lynam *(veteran sports presenter)*

Chris Tarrant *(host of ITV game show,*
Who Wants to Be a Millionaire?*)*

Robert Elms *(radio presenter, BBC London)*

Alexei Sayle *(stand-up comic turned
author and TV producer/presenter)*

RIDING RIDDLES

Guess the bicycle-related solution to this puzzle
Hamlet says not to wear a tailor-made suit while wheeling.

Answer on page 151.

THOMAS HOLDING

Thomas Holding was a prolific writer, tailor, canoeist and a pioneer of leisure camping – he founded the National Camping Club and co-founded CTC. He described the new Saftey bicycle as 'the finest invention of this age' and the ideal escape from the pressures of modern business life in the late 1880s: 'we are hemmed in by routines... by engagements which have to be kept'. But two wheels gives you the 'self-willedness, the abandon, the go-as-you-pleasedness, the freedom of life, its jollity, the independence'.

THOSE WONDERFUL MEN ON THEIR
RUNNING MACHINES

The forerunner to the modern bicycle was patented in 1818 by a German inventor, Karl von Drais. His *laufmaschine* (German for 'running machine'), known in various forms as *draisine*, *draisienne*, or *vélocipède* (French for 'fast foot'), consisted of two wheels connected by a crossbar upon which the rider would sit, propelling himself by scooting his feet along the ground. It was heavy, cumbersome, made entirely of wood, and could travel at around 8mph. Adaptations of this steerable, though far from elegant, contraption soon proved popular in Britain, where it came to be known as the 'hobby horse' or 'dandy horse', due to its particular association with young men of the upper classes, who enjoyed taking it for rides in parks and gardens.

The new-fangled contraption was subject to ridicule in wider society and the press, and its popularity was short-lived, largely due to its unsuitability to longer journeys and rough ground – not to mention the cost of wear-and-tear to riders' shoes. The scornful view expressed by the poet Keats, in a letter dated 13 March 1819, was typical of commentators of the time: 'The nothing of the day is a machine called the *vélocipède*. It is a wheel-carriage to ride cock-horse upon, sitting astride and pushing it along with the toes, a rudder-wheel in hand – they will go seven miles an hour.' Another contemporary report describes how, at the peak of its fashionability, 'hundreds might be seen in a day', but within three years 'the rage had ceased' and the term *vélocipède* had become obsolete in common parlance.

Nevertheless, the early designs were revived and improved upon in later years and eventually evolved – via the boneshaker, the high-wheeled 'ordinary' (penny farthing) and the revolutionary 'safety bicycle' – into the machine we know and love today.

Von Drais's invention has now come full circle, in the form of the kiddies' balance bikes that have surged in popularity in recent years, particularly in northern Europe. As cycling historian Volker Briese observed, if von Drais were with us today, 'he would be happy to see lots of children enthusiastically riding little running machines on park lanes or pavements... never before have so many running machines been produced, sold and ridden'. So, it might be said, the inventor had the last *lauf*...

THE 100 CLUB: CYCLING CLUBS MORE
THAN A CENTURY OLD

Worthing Excelsior Cycling Club (Worthing, Sussex) was founded in 1887 as the Worthing Working Men's Excelsior Cycling Club. About that time, chain-driven 'safety' bicycles were beginning to supersede the high-wheeled ordinary (penny farthing) models, and cycling was no longer the preserve of the wealthy elite; labourers were starting to use bicycles to make the most of their leisure time.

Main activities: time trialling, road racing and touring

Club colours: blue/black/white

Famous members: JP Saville, veteran British mountain biker (successes include silver medal in the 1989 National MTB Championship) and industry pioneer – he helped establish Canada's Kona brand as a market-leader in the UK in the 1980s.

CROWD TROUBLE

In 2006, Tour de France organisers talked of a crackdown on fans taking snapshots on their mobile phones after three crashes in the first five days of the race – including a nasty fall for Sandy Casar, who collided with a drunken spectator who was trying to film the action.

WRITERS ON BICYCLES

We taught ourselves, and may I never forget our earlier rides, through and through Richmond Park when the afternoons were shortest, upon the incomparable Ripley Road when we gave a day to it. Raffles rode a Beeston Humber, a Royal Sunbeam was good enough for me, but he insisted on our both having Dunlop tires: 'They seem the most popular brand. I had my eye on the road all the way from Ripley to Cobham, and there were more Dunlop marks than any other kind. Bless you, yes, they all leave their special tracks, and we don't want ours to be extra special; the Dunlop's like a rattlesnake, and the Palmer leaves telegraph-wires, but surely the serpent is more in our line.'

EW Hornung, 'The Wrong House' (from *Raffles, Further Adventures of the Amateur Cracksman*), 1901

ONLINE CYCLING

A list of popular internet forums devoted to cycling

Roadcycling UK
Want to know which shaving cream is best for shaving legs? This is the place to ask.
www.roadcyclinguk.com

Cycling Plus
Cycling Plus is a general interest cycle magazine, with the focus on road bikes.
www.cyclingplus.co.uk/forum

CTC
Discussion boards of the UK's national cyclists' organisation, CTC, open to non-members; covering everything from campaigns to tour tips.
http://forum.ctc.org.uk

Bikeforums.net
A US-based website with a wide cross-section of topics, and input from UK forum regulars.
www.bikeforums.net

UK Biking
Covers both road cycling and mountain biking.
www.uk-biking.net

Why Cycle
Site geared towards new cyclists and anyone thinking about taking up cycling.
www.whycycle.co.uk

Veloriders
Site with training and technical discussion for time triallists and road and track racers.
www.veloriders.co.uk

Singletrack
A busy forum on the website of British mountain bike magazine, *Singletrack*.
www.singletrackworld.com/forum

What MTB
This site has general mountain bike discussion, including an area for those new to the sport.
www.whatmtb.com/forum

Trials
For everything related to trials (obstacle course) riding, including a guide to equipment and techniques.
www.trials-forum.co.uk/forum

Bikemagic
Site focusing on all aspects of the mountain biking scene and including gear reviews.
www.bikemagic.com

Cyclosport UK
The definitive website for UK sportives, with details on taking part and news from the scene.
www.cyclosport.co.uk

QUOTE UNQUOTE

Even if I did not enjoy riding, I would still do it for my peace of mind. What a wonderful tonic to be exposed to bright sunshine, drenching rain, choking dust, dripping fog, rigid air, punishing winds!
Paul de Vivie, aka 'Velocio' (1853-1930), publisher of *Le Cycliste*

Number of editions of the Giro d'Italia held (up to and including 2006) 89
since the first race in 1909

COMMON CYCLISTS' AFFLICTIONS

Bicycle walk – peculiar, rounded stride of the cyclist when dismounted, as if still pedalling, with a 'pushing off' action when feet come into contact with the ground.

Bicycle back – hunching of the shoulders caused by too much time spent riding in an aerodynamic head-down, bottom-up position.

Bicycle face – a grim set jaw, wild eyes, and strained lines around the mouth as a result of what one observer has described as 'the constant strain to preserve equilibrium'. Particularly evident on steep climbs and sprint finishes.

Bicycle feet – corns, calluses and blisters often result from shoes rubbing at the heels and toes; a properly fitted cycling shoe with a firm sole is advised for comfort on all but the shortest rides.

Bicycle hands – numbness in fingers and thumbs, accompanied by strained wrists, a common complaint among long-distance tourers.

Bicycle bum (saddlesores) – the buttocks and pelvis are the main point of contact between rider and machine, and often the worst-affected parts of the body on long or bumpy rides.

Bicycle knees – most knee problems in cycling (apart from those caused by crashes) are due to improper positioning of the foot and leg. For instance, if the seat is too high, pain may develop in the patella (knee cap) tendon due to over-extension of the leg.

ALTERNATIVE PEDAL POWER

Bicycles are not just about getting from A to B. Pedals and cranks are also used to drive equipment for all manner of work-related activities, from farming to construction, lending new meaning to the expression 'utility cycling'.

Pedal power is not new ('velocipede' machines such as foot-powered lathes and saws were in use in the late 19th century), although it is being used in ever-more diverse ways, particularly as an alternative energy source in the developing world.

One of the best examples is provided by MayaPedal, a non-governmental organisation located in San Andrés Itzapa, Chimaltenango, Guatemala. Since 2001, the initiative has recycled old bikes to build a variety of pedal-powered machines, known collectively as 'bicimáquinas', which are distributed locally for use in peasant agriculture, domestic work and small business.

CYCLING GOLD

The Golden Bike standard is granted by the Union Cycliste Internationale (UCI) to the best 'cycling for all' events – that is, events that any cyclist can enter regardless of skill or experience. The 2007 calendar consisted of nine events in nine countries – seven in Europe, one in South Africa and one in New Zealand – chosen to give riders 'the opportunity to discover the best races in the world':

Cape Argus Pick 'n Pay Cycle Tour, South Africa *(March)*

De Ronde van Vlaanderen, Belgium *(April)*

Toerversie Amstel Gold Race, Netherlands *(April)*

Gran Fondo Internazionale Felice Gimondi, Italy *(May)*

Quebrantahuesos, Spain *(June)*

Cyclosportive l'Ariégeoise, France *(June)*

Gruyère Cycling Tour, Switzerland *(August)*

Rothaus RiderMan, Germany *(September)*

Wattyl Lake Taupo Cycle Challenge, New Zealand *(November)*

THE CYCLING EVANGELIST

If confirmation were ever needed that cycling brings one closer to God, it comes surely in the form of Ion Keith-Falconer, a world champion cyclist and Christian preacher.

Keith-Falconer was born into a Scottish aristocratic family, and after an education at Harrow School and Cambridge University (where he studied theology), he went on to distinguish himself as an Arabic scholar of international repute.

He still found time, however, to pursue an outstanding career as an amateur cyclist and as a missionary at home and abroad, particularly the Middle East.

His height (6ft 3in) enabled him to ride high-wheeled penny farthings, or ordinary bicycles, with a wheel span of 62 inches.

His cycling successes included beating professional champion John Keen over two miles in 1878, and winning the 50-mile Bicycle Union amateur championship race at Crystal Palace in 1882, when he set a new record of 2 hours, 43 minutes and 55.2 seconds. In the same year, he made an unprecedented 994-mile ride from Land's End to John O'Groats in 13 days.

His sporting fame no doubt attracted many to his preaching missions in London. A report in the *Weekly Dispatch* (August 1879) reported on his joining the evangelist movement, and stated that 'his reputation as a bicyclist has drawn many in who would not otherwise have come within sound of the gospel'.

Estimated number of summer cycle trips made in 2002 by riders 91 in the US

Downhill speed biking

If you thought the piste was reserved for skiers and snowboarders, think again. As if to prove the point that there is nowhere on Earth that man cannot travel on a humble bicycle, a select band of speed-freaks have, in recent years, taken the sport of downhill mountain biking to the world's fastest ski slopes.

The result? Gravity, ice, pedal power and the latest technology combine to produce the fastest speeds possible on two unmotorised wheels – and, it might be argued, the most frightening thing you can do on a bike without breaking the law.

Speed-bikers ride their specially adapted machines – featuring aerodynamic fairings and spiked tyres – down a 60-degree, snow-covered slope at more than 125mph (in 1998, Frenchman Christian Taillefer set a world record when he sped down a glacier at 132mph). The riders themselves are kitted out in skin-tight, all-in-one suits and wildly decorated, oversized helmets that make them look as though they have just touched down from outer space. Their fearlessness in pursuit of ever-greater speeds certainly marks them out as an alien species of cyclist.

QUOTE UNQUOTE

When I go out with someone for the first time I immediately glance at his legs to know how fast we're going to go and with what sauce I'm going to be eaten. You can read a cyclist by his legs.
Paul Fournel, author, *Need for the Bike*

WRITERS ON BICYCLES

Very soon, alas! the sexes will be robbed of one of the first and most thrilling motives of romance, the motive of *As You Like It*, the romance of wearing each other's clothes. Alas, that every advance of reason should mean a corresponding retreat of romance! It is only reasonable that woman, being – have you yet realised the fact? – a biped like her brothers, should, when she takes to her brothers' recreations, dress as those recreations demand; and yet the death of Rosalind is a heavy price to pay for the lady bicyclist. So soon as the two sexes wear the same clothes, they may as well wear nothing; the game of sex is up. In this matter, as in others, we cannot both have our cake and eat it.

Richard le Gallienne, *Quest of the Golden Girl*, 1897

92 *Length in feet according to the* Guinness World Records *book, of the world's longest bicycle, built by engineering students in the Netherlands*

ALL HAIL THE TAXI CYCLE

Taxi cycles are relatively new in the UK, but other countries cottoned on long ago. Here are the figures for the number of cargo and taxi cycles used across the world.

India	1.7 million
China	750,000
Bangladesh	700,000
Indonesia	300,000
Vietnam	150,000
Colombia	100,000
Chile	100,000
Burma	60,000
Nepal	50,000
Europe	20,000

RIDING RIDDLES

Cyclist A passes a milestone at 11am, travelling at 10mph. Cyclist B passes the same milestone 15 minutes later travelling at 15mph. At what time will B catch up with A?

Answer on page 151.

TIME FOR TEA

A good cup of tea and a slice of cake can revive flagging spirits on even the longest and wettest of countryside tours; for this reason many cycling clubs keep detailed records of bike-friendly cafés on their local runs.

Worthy of special mention is the Impromptu Tea Room in Elsdon, Northumberland, which has a long tradition of serving cyclists on long-distance rides across the Pennines.

Known for cheap yet tasty home cooking, and situated in a former school house dating back to the early 1700s, the Impromptu has wonderful views across the village of Elsdon and the surrounding hills. It also doubles as an official information point for the Northumberland National Park.

In a review for the Speedwell Bicycle Club, one rider describes the Impromptu as 'the best cyclists' café I ever visited... the atmosphere was definitely communal. We sat at long tables on bench seats and the owners kept bringing large pots of tea, which they placed on the tables for all to help themselves to unlimited quantities'.

Running time in minutes of the DVD Maestro: The Reg Harris Story, 93 a documentary on Britain's first cycling superstar

A CYCLE WEDDING AT WISBECH

The following is a local newspaper report of a wedding that took place in Wisbech, Cambridgeshire, on 21 April 1897. The photograph in the original article shows the bride and groom riding side by side on a 'sociable' – an exotic machine described in as much detail as the bride's dress.

'St Augustine's Church, and its vicinity, together with the Lynn Road, were crowded with people on Wednesday afternoon last, the attraction being a "cycle wedding". The bridegroom was Mr UD Palmer, of the Borough Cycle Works, and the bride Miss FM Stevenson, third daughter of Mr CF Stevenson late of Tydd and now of Norfolk Street East.

'The wedding is the first of its kind in the district which accounted for the large attendance of spectators. The ceremony was fixed for two o'clock, and shortly before that time, the bridegroom and best man rode upon a Rudge Whitworth companion or sociable bicycle. This machine is the first to be introduced into the district and the announcement that the bride and bridegroom would ride together on the machine through the town was the cause of the interest displayed by the public.

'Shortly after the bridegroom had reached the church, the bride and bridesmaids arrived on safety bicycles. The bride wore a blue grey dress trimmed with white chiffon, a white tulle hat, trimmed with ostrich tips and Moire ribbon, and carried a handsome bouquet of white flowers and maiden hair fern.

'On emerging from the church, Mr & Mrs Palmer were received with showers of confetti and rice. The sociable bicycle was near at hand and the newly-married couple at once mounted it and rode off in the direction of the bride's father's home in Norfolk St East, followed by the best man and the bridesmaids on bicycles.

'The presents were numerous and useful, and included a handsome tea service from the committee of the Wisbech Bicycle Club, of which the bridegroom is a member.

'This "bicycle made for two" upon which the couple rode from church is a great novelty in itself. There are only two wheels, similar to an ordinary safety bicycle, and the riders sit side by side. The machine is automatically balanced, and is fitted with Palmer tyres. All the parts of the machine are plated and it is enamelled in tan colour, lined out with gold. Although the riders sit side by side there is no inconvenience felt if one rider is heavier than the other, and a good rider could take up a novice for a partner who had never ridden a bicycle before.'

OLD PICTURE, NEW CAPTION

POUNDBURY CAMP
on the Frome.

*Alan's idea of a shortcut to beat the
others had backfired majorly.*

READ ALL ABOUT IT

Ten best-selling books about cycle touring and trail-riding

1. *Cycling in the UK: The Official Guide to the National Cycle Network*, by Sandi Toksvig, Nick Cotton and John Grimshaw
2. *French Revolutions: Cycling the Tour de France*, by Tim Moore
3. *Bike Britain: Cycling from Land's End to John O'Groats*, by Paul Salter
4. *Mountainbike Scotland: The Highlands (Vol 1)* , by Kenny Wilson
5. *Philip's Cycle Tours: Kent and Sussex*
6. *AA 40 Pub Walks & Cycle Rides: South Downs & the South Coast*
7. *White Peak Mountain Biking: The Pure Trails*, by Jon Barton
8. *Lake District Mountain Biking*, by Richard Staton and Chris Gore
9. *Downhill All the Way: Cycling Through France from La Manche to the Mediterranean*, by Edward Enfield
10. *South West Mountain Biking: Quantocks, Exmoor, Dartmoor Trail Guide*, by Nick Cotton

---

THE HOLY TRAIL – A GUIDE FOR PEDALLING PILGRIMS

Notre-Dame des Cyclistes, Aquitaine, France

'Mary, Queen of the world, we humbly ask you to bless and protect the cyclists of the world and help them to finish happily the main and final stage, which leads to heaven. Amen.'

So reads the inscription at the feet of a statue of the Virgin Mother outside Notre-Dame des Cyclistes, an 11th-century chapel (originally Notre-Dame de Géou) near the small medieval village La Bastide d'Armagnac.

The chapel's association with cycling goes back to the 1950s, when the priest – a self-confessed Tour de France obsessive – had the idea of creating a site of pilgrimage for cyclists, apparently following the example of the Italian cyclists' church, the Madonna del Ghisallo.

Notre-Dame des Cyclistes was inaugurated by the Vatican in 1959, and since then has become a holy repository of bikes, jerseys and other collectibles donated by famous riders.

One of the highlights of any pilgrim's visit is the stained-glass window – a rainbow-coloured representation of Mary – designed by French rider Henry Anglade (second in the 1959 Tour de France).

CYCLING IN VERSE

A few poems that feature cycling

'Church Going', by Philip Larkin (*'Hatless, I take off/My cycle-clips in awkward reverence'*)

'The Commander', by John Betjeman (*'As bicycling we went/By saffron-spotted palings to crumbling box-paved churches/Down hazel lanes in Kent'*)

'To You', by Kenneth Koch (*'I think I am bicycling across an Africa of green and white fields/Always, to be near you, even in my heart'*)

'Anxiety', by DH Lawrence (*'Along the vacant road, a red/Bicycle approaches'*)

'Poor Fellows', by Pablo Neruda (*'Till a man and his girl have to raise their climax/Full tilt/On a bicycle'*)

'The Shut-Eye Sentry', by Rudyard Kipling (*"E's usin' 'is sword for a bicycle, but, sentry, shut your eye"*)

He was pedalling slowly in the middle of the street, reading a newspaper which he held with both hands spread open before his eyes. Every now and then he rang his bell without interrupting his reading. I watched him recede till he was no more than a dot on the horizon.

Samuel Beckett, 'The Calmative',
in *Stories and Texts for Nothing*, 1967

A SPECTATOR'S GUIDE TO CYCLE SPORT

Mountain biking

There are four main disciplines in competitive mountain biking: downhill, four cross (4X), cross country and trials. All are contested at the annual Mountain Biking World Championships, the biggest event in the off-road calendar.

Downhill, as its name suggests, is all about speed. Races only last a few minutes, and for competitors it is primarily a test of nerves and bike control; riding individually against the clock, they hurtle down a steep downhill gradient over jumps, bumps, berms (cambered corners) and drop-offs – often descending several hundred metres in the space of a two-mile course.

Four Cross is a variation of downhill racing in which four riders compete against each other over an obstacle-strewn course. The start is controlled by a BMX-style mechanical gate. Physical contact and crashes are frequent and, on well-designed courses, four cross is arguably the most action-packed of all cycle sports from a spectator's point of view.

The key to **cross-country** riding – the only mountain-biking event to have featured in the Olympic games at the time of publication – is physical endurance rather than technical prowess. Events usually have a massed start, and top riders can maintain average speeds of 12mph over a typical two-hour race despite the bone-shaking terrain.

For the highest level of pure bike-handling skill and athleticism, **trials** competitors are the ones to watch. The object is to ride over obstacle courses ('sections') without putting a foot down. Obstacles can include anything from rocks and shrubs to tables and cars. The rider with the fewest penalty points is declared the winner.

CYCLISTS' CHARTER

London's evening newspaper, the *Evening Standard*, a publication traditionally supportive of motorists' rights, had a sudden change of heart in April 2007. Amid detailed coverage of the problems facing the city's wheelers, the paper launched a campaign for safer cycling based on a '12-point charter for cyclists' – containing demands that many would like to see implemented in towns and cities across the UK:

1. A real cycle network across London
2. Better cycle lanes with proper segregation
3. Enforcement of special advanced stop lines for cyclists
4. Heavy goods vehicles (HGVs) to be fitted with special cyclist safety mirrors
5. Compulsory cyclist awareness training for all bus drivers and new HGV drivers
6. Cycle-friendly streets: fewer one-way systems that funnel cyclists into the middle of traffic
7. More cycle parking across London
8. A police crackdown on bike theft
9. Make safe the Thames bridges: some of the most dangerous places for cyclists
10. Campaign to alert the self-employed that they can claim a 20p a mile cycling allowance against tax
11. Better cycle-bus-rail coordination; adequate parking at all railway stations
12. Cycle training for all schoolchildren and any adult who wants it

BICYCLE BOMBERS

In the days leading up to the start of World War II, the IRA launched one of its first attacks on the UK mainland: a bicycle bomb in Coventry, the traditional heartland of the English bicycle industry.

Five people were killed and 100 injured in the explosion, caused by a bomb left in the basket of a tradesman's bicycle, and the attack prompted a strike by workers in the city, protesting at 'having to work with Irish labour', according to a contemporary report.

Bicycle bombs were also a feature of conflict in Vietnam, as documented in the novel *The Quiet American*, by Graham Greene. More recently, bicycle bombs have been detonated by rebel groups in cities in Pakistan, Iraq and Afghanistan – often with large numbers of fatalities and casualties among civilians and security forces.

98 *Percentage of children in England who do not cycle to school, according to a 2005 study*

EXTREME CYCLING

Underwater cycling

Underwater cycling is a lesser-known 'sport of kings'; Lord Louis Mountbatten was the first (and quite possibly the last) member of the royal family to try the sport, and his attempt was captured on film off the coast of Malta in the 1950s. The highly specialised sport will always be a fringe affair – participants wear scuba gear and need to be qualified sea divers as well as strong cyclists – but in recent years its reach has begun to spread. Since the mid-1990s, an annual underwater competition has been held in the sea off Beaufort, North Carolina. In 2005, a sub-aqua race was held in Guernsey as part of national celebrations to mark the 200th anniversary of the Battle of Trafalgar. A field of international competitors rode from St Peter Port's Havelet Bay to Castle Cornet – a distance of around 250m – setting a Guinness World Record for the world's largest underwater cycling event. The Guernsey 'Soumarine' race is now held annually.

EARLY CYCLING DITTIES

Is it possible to be too attached to one's bicycle? Perhaps so, judging by this vengeful ditty. The message to the 'miscreant' who wrote off the author's tricycle was penned on 'two sleepless nights following the disaster' and published in the journal of the Cyclists' Touring Club journal, in 1879. Interestingly, the writer manages to coin no less than three terms for bike murder.

What punishment such crime can wait?
In agony I cried –
What retribution be thy fate?
Thou vile Bicyclicide!!

Had'st crushed at first thy shallow fate,
Thou had'st not earned beside,
My triple scorn, and three-fold hate
O fell Tricyclicide!!

Thy crime, upon the Rolls of Fame
For ever shall abide;
Thy sin shall be itself thy shame;
I brand thee with the awful name –
Velocipedicide!!

**To the Miscreant Who Ruined my Tricycle,
'HCH', 1897**

BACKPEDALLING

Cycling museums, archives and collections in the UK

National Cycle Archive
Location: Modern Records Centre, University of Warwick, Coventry
Highlights include: Books, magazines and records deposited by numerous cycling bodies and individuals, with its largest archive coming from CTC.
www2.warwick.ac.uk/services/library/mrc

The National Cycle Collection
Location: Llandrindod Wells, Powys, Mid Wales
Highlights include: C.1881 Royal Salvo Tricycle (similar to the machine presented to Queen Victoria), 65 classic and touring bicycles from 1940-1980, 1,500 club badges alphabetically arranged and framed, and an Isaac Force 2005 Shimano Dura Ace 10 equipped complete racing bike, weighing just 16lb.
www.cyclemuseum.org.uk

British Cycling Museum
Location: The Old Station, Camelford, Cornwall
Highlights include: Old-fashioned cycle repair workshop, more than 1,000 cycling medals, fobs and badges from 1881, and the first bicycle oil lamp.
www.chycor.co.uk/cycling-museum

Science Museum Swindon
Location: Wroughton, Swindon
Highlights include: The Lotus bike on which Chris Boardman won an individual pursuit gold medal at the 1992 Barcelona Summer Olympics.
www.sciencemuseumswindon.org.uk

Coventry Transport Museum
Location: Hales Street, Coventry
Highlights include: The Cyclopedia Gallery is devoted to the museum's cycle collection. Visitors can sit on replica 'boneshakers', penny farthings and hobby horses and race on high-tech training machines.
www.transport-museum.com

Cycle Exhibition, Amberley Working Museum
Location: Amberley, West Sussex
Highlights include: An 1860s 'boneshaker', a penny-farthing from the 1870s, and a recreation of a 1920s cycle repair shop.
www.amberleymuseum.co.uk

QUOTE UNQUOTE

All cyclists quickly make up their own bestiary. My own list of the most hateful drivers in London ends with one particular car, the Mercedes, since it seems to attract people not merely blind to bikes but homicidal towards them.
Jeremy Paxman, broadcaster and writer, *London Cyclist*

THE CAR'S THE STAR

Miles covered on British roads by vehicle type 1997-2005

	1997	1998	1999	2000	2001	2002	2003	2004	2005
Pedal cycle	41	40	41	42	42	44	45	42	44
Motorcycle	40	41	45	46	48	51	56	52	54
Car/taxi	3,658	3,706	3,774	3,768	3,828	3,929	3,930	3,981	3,972
Bus/coach	52	52	53	52	52	52	54	52	52
LGV	486	509	516	523	536	550	579	608	626
HGV	269	277	281	282	281	283	285	294	290

(unit: 100 million vehicle kilometres)

RIDING RIDDLES

A cyclist riding along a deserted lane came to a crossroad and did not know which way to take. Looking around he saw a four-armed signpost lying on the ground knocked out by a careless motorist. He had a brainwave which enabled him to take the right way. What was it?

Answer on page 151.

SEX AND CYCLING

Mind over matter

Does the act of cycling impart unusual sexual powers on the rider? Perhaps that is what happened in the case of Guy Compton, an Arizona cycle tour leader at the centre of a recent court case in which it was claimed that he could make a woman climax using only his mind. Such is the tale told by the litigant Quoc Pham, who sued his former lover Neli Petkova for running off with Mr Compton – whom she met on a cycling holiday. In a lawsuit filed in Manhattan Supreme Court, Pham demanded $1 million from Petkova, accusing her of duping him into getting her pregnant then dumping him after meeting Compton. But it was cyclist Compton who attracted all the tabloid headlines. '[Petkova] returned from a 10-day guided bicycle trip [in 2003] and told [Pham] that she had met someone else that could make her cervix orgasmic just by thinking and that [Pham] was sexually inadequate,' the lawsuit stated. Lucky chap... most cyclists would settle for being able to change a tyre without using their hands.

Number of units in millions that worldwide bicycle production 101 exceeded in 2000

Children aged 11 to 15 cycle more than any other age group in the UK, according to a recent study by the National Children's Bureau. Cycling is also among the most popular sport-related activities pursued out of school: a Sport England survey on children's physical activity found that 51% of six- to 16-year-olds regularly take part in extra-curricular swimming, 49% cycle, and 37% play football.

Promising figures – until they are put into broader historical context. The last two or three decades have seen a dramatic fall in the distance cycled by children and young people under 16 years of age – a drop of about 40% for boys and more than 50% for girls. Furthermore, there is a large gulf in the level of cycling between the sexes: boys, on average, cover 138 miles a year, girls just 24.

Perhaps the most telling statistic is that only 1% of primary schoolchildren and 2% of secondary schoolchildren cycle to school in the UK – which compares woefully to countries such as Denmark and the Netherlands. And, despite the popularity of extra-curricular cycling, it is the sport that children are least likely to be offered in PE lessons – behind volleyball and baseball.

While the government is unlikely to make cycling a compulsory part of the national curriculum, it has gone some way to redress the balance in recent years by providing £15 million for initiatives aimed at getting more kids on bikes. These include Bikeability, a new award scheme, described as 'the cycling proficiency test for the 21st century'. The ultimate goal is to ensure that no child leaves primary school without being offered formal cycle training.

Perhaps the nation is finally waking up to the fact that the lack of free-wheeling exercise impacts not only on the health of young people – something that we are constantly reminded of in newspaper headlines about obesity – but also their spirit.

As the National Children's Bureau report concluded: 'Cycling for children sometimes has a playful, exploratory character that is rarely present in adult cycling. When children are given free rein to cycle in their free time – common even today in countries with high levels of cycling and common a decade or two ago in the UK – unplanned wanderings and cycling for fun feature strongly.'

OLD PICTURE, NEW CAPTION

*A group of ladies wading in the stream below engaged
Edward in polite conversation, unaware that the mad old
fruit was completely naked from the waist down.*

HINTS ON CYCLING TO HOUNDS

Many hunt followers today use bicycles to keep up with the pack, but they would likely be hounded out themselves if they tried to join the chase. Not so in 1907, judging by a treatise written by the Reverend W Gresswell in *The Badminton Magazine* (a popular sporting journal of the day).

'When governed by a true sporting instinct the cyclist after hounds need not be an unpopular adjunct to a hunt; on the contrary, he will be not only welcomed, but respected by any Master of Hounds,' wrote the Reverend.

His article, entitled 'Hints on cycling to hounds', offered the following sound advice to those wishing to follow his own example: 'When cycling in a run, and horses are galloping behind you, never slow down or get off suddenly. I saw a cyclist do that once with nearly fatal results... Keep perfectly cool and ride straight, and horsemen will see how to avoid you. In riding a cycle with hounds you need a good nerve, great discernment, great judgment, and plenty of discretion. All this combined with a quick eye to see a sudden turn of things and an inherent genius for guessing a fox's movements will enable a man to extract an enormous amount of enjoyment from a day with the hounds...'

HOW TO FIT A HELMET

a) Measure the head around its circumference, about one inch above the eyebrows. Match your head size to the size of the helmet (printed in the helmet, on a label or on the box).

b) Place the helmet squarely on your head and fasten the straps. If it's loose, use the pads or straps to get a close fit. It should feel snug all the way around, but not too tight.

c) Once the pads are fitted, place the helmet back on your head. Keep it level, about one inch above the eyebrows, and adjust the outside straps so there is no slackness.

d) The front strap should be as vertical as possible. The rear strap should join the front strap just under the ears.

e) Fasten the buckle, which should rest under the chin, not on the jaw line.

f) Try to move the helmet on your head. It should not move very much.

g) Helmets with peaks at the front help keep the rain off the rider's face, but they are not recommended for urban roads as the peak can obscure your view of traffic signals.

ENGLAND'S BEST KNOWN, UNKNOWN ARTIST

The illustrations of Frank Patterson (1871-1952), a master of cycling art, adorned the pages of magazines such as *Cycling*, and most first appeared in CTC's *Cycle* magazine.

Patterson – or 'Pat' – was a keen cyclist in his youth, but a leg injury when he was 38 curtailed his riding. He had so absorbed cycling lore, however, that his drawings made a huge impact on tourists, clubmen and racers alike.

The bucolic scenes – often serene, sometimes whimsical and occasionally gloomy – capture lone cyclists, or tourers in pairs, wheeling through rolling countryside or stopping at a welcoming village hostelry for refreshment. Although he produced some 26,000 line drawings during his lifetime – you can see many used throughout this book – little of his work in oils and watercolours remains.

Despite a loyal following among cyclists and fellow artists, his works did not receive the wider recognition many felt he deserved; the Frank Patterson Society refers to him as 'England's best known, unknown artist'.

CYCLE COUTURE

Rapha

There are many companies that make good technical gear, but few can match the sense of road race-inspired style and passion ingrained in every stitch of clothing produced by the London-based label, Rapha (the name comes from a legendary French cycling team from the 1960s – St Raphael – led by five-times Tour de France winner Jacques Anquetil). The emphasis is on traditions established on the continent – and taken firmly to heart by British road racers – in the golden age of post-war road cycling, from classic club-style jerseys and caps to fixed shorts ('tailored plus fours for urban riding'). It is one of the few cycle clothing companies whose products regularly appear in the glossy pages of newspaper fashion supplements and men's style magazines such as *GQ*, and it produces its own high-end cycling journal, *Rouleur*, 'to celebrate the drama and beauty of road racing'. In the space of a few years, Rapha has established itself as a firm favourite with the aesthetically astute (and monied) members of the cycling fraternity. This reputation was sealed in 2005 when, as commercial partner to the Tour of Britain, Rapha supplied race wear for senior officials, and the company's iconic 1940s Citroen 'H' van was used as the *voiture balai*, the 'broom wagon' that follows the peloton to sweep up abandoned riders. The average bike messenger, it's fair to say, is unlikely to be decked out in a limited edition jersey (£175, produced in partnership with the designer Paul Smith), but a select few London couriers do, at least, get to try out new items as part of the company's tough road-testing regime.

WORLD WAR I: THE FIRST CASUALTY

Private John Parr, the first British soldier killed in enemy action on the Western Front, was a reconnaissance cyclist for the 4th Battalion Middlesex Regiment. At the start of hostilities in August 1914, as the German army marched into Belgium, Parr's unit took up position alongside a canal running through the town of Mons. On 21 August, Parr and another man were sent as a two-man cycle patrol to the village of Obourg, just north-east of Mons, with a mission to locate the enemy. It is believed that they came across a cavalry patrol from the German First Army, and Parr remained to hold off the enemy while his companion returned to report. He was killed in the ensuing rifle fire.

On a bike your consciousness is small. The harder you work, the smaller it gets. Every thought that arises is immediately and utterly true, every unexpected event is something you'd known all along but had only forgotten for a moment. A pounding riff from a song, a bit of long division that starts over and over, a magnified anger at someone, is enough to fill your thoughts.

During the race, what goes round in the rider's mind is a monolithic ball bearing, so smooth, so uniform, that you can't even see it spin. Its almost perfect lack of surface structure ensures that it strikes nothing that might end up in the white circulation of thought. Almost nothing, that is – sometimes a microscopic flaw manages to strike a chord. From race number 203 (evening criterium at Groot Ammers, May 30, 1975) I remember the sound brr-ink, pronounced as two syllables, that popped into my mind every time at the same street corner, twenty, thirty, sixty laps long, that I ruminated over, the way tongue and teeth can play with a half-forgotten wad of gum, a feature film long, until I was back at that corner and brr-ink was refreshed in its original form.

Why not some other corner? Why brr-ink? We know little of the workings of the human mind, as a mass murderer's lawyer once told the courtroom.

I once gave myself the assignment of inventing a completely random word. Completely random, is that possible? And all of a sudden, there it was: Battoowoo Greekgreek.

Battoowoo Greekgreek. Is that a name? I don't know anyone who answers to that. No one will ever be able to tell me where Battoowoo Greekgreek came from. A few million years of evolution haven't resulted in brains that can understand themselves.

Tim Krabbé,
The Rider, 1978

CROWD TROUBLE

In 1975, Eddy Merckx was forced off his bike after being punched in the kidneys by a spectator – possibly a French fan who wanted to prevent the Belgian winning a sixth Tour. He completed the race, but came in two minutes, 47 seconds behind the winner, Bernard Thévenet.

THE BICYCLE: A TRIUMPH OF TECHNOLOGY

In 2005, the BBC's *Reith Lectures* (a series of televised presentations on popular science), tackled 'The Triumph of Technology'. To coincide with the lectures, the Radio 4 discussion programme *You and Yours* set up an online poll to find out what listeners considered to be 'the most significant technological innovation since 1800'.

A shortlist of 10 items was drawn up, based on hundreds of initial nominations from the public and the opinions of five experts. More than 4,500 people voted – but it was a clear victory for the bicycle, which won more than half of the vote based on its simplicity of design, universal use, and because it is an ecologically sound means of transport.

The inventions in order of popularity were as follows:
59.4% – Bicycle
7.8% – Transistor
7.8% – Electro-magnetic induction ring
6.3% – Computer
4.6% – Germ theory of infection
4.5% – Radio
4.0% – Internet
3.4% – Internal combustion engine
1.1% – Nuclear power
1.1% – Communications satellite

BRIDGES FOR BICYCLES

The longest cyclable bridge in the world is believed to be the Chain of Rocks Bridge, with a span of 5,353ft over the Mississippi River, on the north edge of St Louis, Missouri, US. Originally a motor route converted to carry cycling and pedestrian trails, the bridge was the most famous crossing of Route 66 over the Mississippi.

The Big Dam Bridge in Arkansas, US, is the world's longest purpose-built pedestrian and bicycle bridge. The 4,300ft bridge rises up to 90ft above the Arkansas River. It took eight years to build and cost $12.5 million.

Every year, thousands of cyclists cross 14 of London's most historic bridges in one day as part of a charity fund-raising ride. The Stroke Association's annual Thames Bridges Bike Ride, first held in 1994, covers 32 miles, starting at London's City Hall and finishing at Hurst Park, near Hampton Court, in Surrey.

UP, UP AND AWAY!

The Electric Brae is a stretch of road in Ayrshire, Scotland, with seemingly magical properties that allow cyclists to freewheel uphill.

If you want to experience the uniquely unnerving sensation of sitting on your bike at the bottom of a hill, then feeling your steed slowly begin to pull upward under its own steam, head for the A719 (south of Dunure, heading east towards Maybole).

If, however, you are curious to know exactly what bedevils the place, here is the explanation inscribed on a stone at the site:

'The "Electric Brae", known locally as Croy Brae. This runs the quarter mile from the bend overlooking Croy railway viaduct in the west (286 feet above ordnance datum) to the wooded Craigencroy Glen (303 feet above AOD) to the east. Whilst there is this slope of 1 in 86 upwards from the bend at the Glen, the configuration of the land on either side of the road provides an optical illusion making it look as if the slope is going the other way.

'Therefore, a stationary car on the road with the brakes off will appear to move slowly uphill. The term "Electric Brae" dates from a time when it was incorrectly thought to be a phenomenon caused by electric or magnetic attraction within the Brae.'

OLYMPIC RECORD

Cycling has been part of the Olympics since 1896. It is one of only five sports to have been included in every modern Olympics. The others are swimming, athletics, gymnastics and fencing.

CYCLING ON THE CITY WALLS

It is often said that going to the refined Italian city of Lucca and not cycling around its tree-lined walls is like going to Paris and failing to take in the Eiffel Tower. Lucca, in the Tuscany region, is famed for its almost perfectly preserved medieval walls, wide enough to contain beautiful parks and – at one time – a car racing track. Today, the ramparts carry a network of cycle paths on a three-mile circuit that provides the perfect way to see the city. There are bike rental shops all over the city, and two-wheelers are also the best way to get around the narrow streets of the old city centre, which is now largely free of cars.

Useful websites featuring maps, route guides and journey planners

Forestry Commission
Searchable database of 2,600km of cycle trails in National Forests.
www.forestry.gov.uk/cycling

National Cycle Network
Maps and details of around 100 routes, spanning some 10,000 miles.
www.sustrans.org.uk

The National Byway
A 4,500-mile, signposted 'heritage trail' around Britain for cyclists.
www.thenationalbyway.org

CTC maps
Database of routes, plus details of 'obstructions', and the Cyclists Welcome guide to cafés, hotels and bike shops.
www.ctc-maps.org.uk

Local cycle maps directory
A UK list of local authority maps for cyclists.
www.pindar.com/cyclemaps

Life Cycle maps
The Resources section lists more than 70 maps for routes in London, Bristol Sheffield and many other cities. Most can be ordered for free.
www.lifecycleuk.org.uk

London Cycle Network
Mapping service.
www.londoncyclenetwork.org. uk/webmap/default.asp

Transport for London
Downloadable guides and online journey planner.
www.tfl.gov.uk/tfl/roadusers/ cycling/cycleroutes/default.asp

Bikely
Contains more than 12,000 routes around the world – including 1,000 in the UK – logged by cyclists. Routes can be viewed online, printed or downloaded for a Global Positioning System (GPS) device.
www.bikely.com

Gmap pedometer
Distance and calorie calculator designed for runners, but used by many cyclists.
www.gmap-pedometer.com

QUOTE UNQUOTE

When the spirits are low, when the day appears dark, when work becomes monotonous, when hope hardly seems worth having, just mount a bicycle and go out for a spin down the road, without thought on anything but the ride you are taking.
Arthur Conan Doyle, author

THE 100 CLUB: CYCLING CLUBS MORE THAN A CENTURY OLD

The Speedwell Bicycle Club (Feckenham, Worcestershire), founded in May 1876, claims to be one of the oldest extant cycling clubs in the world. Its name comes from the street where founding members met (Speedwell Road, Edgbaston).

Main activities: time trialling and road racing, as well as a regular series of club runs and social events

Club colours: claret and blue – based on the strip of the local football club, Aston Villa

Famous members: Sir Alfred Bird (1849–1922), food manufacturer (the family business was built on the success of Bird's custard powder) and MP for Wolverhampton West, who set a record for tricycling from Land's End to John O' Groats.

STAMP OF APPROVAL

Cycling stamps issued by the Royal Mail

1978: *Centenaries of CTC and the British Cycling Federation*
Four stamps were issued to mark the double anniversary, featuring bicycles from different eras: 'Penny-farthing and 1884 Safety Bicycle' (9p), '1920 Touring Bicycles' ($10^1/_2$p), 'Modern Small-wheel Bicycles' (11p), and '1978 Road Racers' (13p).

1999: *Liberation by Bike*
Part of a special series of 48 stamps to mark the Millennium, each one designed by a British artist and celebrating something that had been achieved in Britain during the previous century. Stamp number 43 – with a value of 26p – was 'Liberation by Bike', a vivid, red and gold design showing a winged female cyclist flying along on the first ladies' safety bicycle. The illustration evokes the new freedoms that the chain-driven bicycle, which was much easier to ride than the penny farthing, offered women of the time.

2000: *Cycle Network Artworks*
This 45p stamp was issued as part of the Millennium Collection, and commemorated the opening of the National Cycle Network in June that year. As part of its launch, the network also hosted the country's biggest collection of outdoor public art, with various works spread across 5,000 miles of tracks across the UK.

CYCLE CAMPING

Some cyclists baulk at the idea of taking anything more than their clothes and their wallet with them on a biking tour; these 'credit card' tourers simply pay for accommodation, food and supplies as and when they need to on their journey, to keep baggage to an absolute minimum. For those who prefer to go fully prepared, here is a basic list of what you will need; you might want to add luxuries such as a radio and camera equipment if you have space.

- Clothing (including warm layers and waterproofs)
- Tent and ground mat
- Sleeping bag (in waterproof bag)
- Cooking gear (gas stove and fuel, pot, cutlery set, sharp knife, matches, can opener)
- Food and water (including lots of energy bars for snacking on the move)
- Tools (pump, puncture repair kit, small screwdrivers, wrenches, allen keys, pliers, chain tool, spoke tool, crank extractor, freewheel removers)
- Spares (tyres, inner tubes, spokes, cables, rear axle)
- Personal items (scissors, mirror, comb, toothbrush, soap, towel, sun cream, lip balm, tissues, toilet paper)
- Bike lock
- Notebook and pen
- Compass
- Torch and batteries
- Mobile phone (for emergencies)
- Road maps in watertight pouch

A SPECTATOR'S GUIDE TO CYCLE SPORT

Bicycle Polo

Bike polo was invented by Irishman Richard J Mecredy in 1891 – just under 20 years after the Hurlingham Club set the modern rules for equestrian polo. In July 1908, it featured as a demonstration sport at the London Olympics (Ireland beat Germany 3-1 in the final) and, by 1938, the Bicycle Polo Association of Great Britain could boast 170 teams in 100 clubs, with more than 1,000 players. The sport never regained momentum following World War II, however. Today it is something of a fringe sport, though the International Bicycle Polo Federation (member countries include Great Britain, Ireland, India and the US) was formed in 1996 in an attempt to revive its fortunes.

A cycling demonstration town is a place where people ride their bikes in formation every day – where ranks of cyclist citizens bring joy to passers-by with coordinated displays of trick riding, like a massed, wheeled version of the famous flying Red Arrows...

...if only. The bad news is that England is not quite ready for such a free-wheeling fantasia, but the good news is that it is ready for a £17 million programme to boost cycling by creating six bike-friendly towns.

According to Cycling England, the national body that is overseeing the scheme, the selected towns are using the money (allocated over a three-year period to 2008) to develop 'an exemplary physical environment for cycling'.

So if you are a cyclist in the following towns, count your blessings. Everyone else will have to wait for the government to make cycling a national priority when it comes to transport planning (tip: don't hold your breath).

AYLESBURY

One of the main cycle route developments is a new £5 million bridge over the railway to the town centre and residential areas, open to both cyclists and walkers.

BRIGHTON & HOVE

Work has started on a regional cycle route from Hove to Hangleton, and the council's programme has been offering residents free bicycle maintenance courses, cycle training, maps and guides.

DARLINGTON

A major construction to create a 'pedestrian heart' in Darlington is underway – out go cars and buses and in come cyclists and pedestrians. In future, traffic will only be allowed into the town centre at night.

DERBY

Projects include the R66 Cycle Ringway, due for completion at the end of 2007, ensuring that everyone in the city is within two miles of a main cycle route.

EXETER

Work is underway on the £6 million development of the Exe Estuary route. The estuary will eventually have cycle paths down both sides as far as Exmouth on the east side and Dawlish on the west.

LANCASTER WITH MORECAMBE

The funding helped create a change in a local by-law so that cyclists can ride on Morecambe Bay promenade, which was formerly restricted to pedestrians.

OLD PICTURE, NEW CAPTION

*Lionel was still a bit miffed at being over-charged for
an inner-tube, so he decided to go back to the shop
and put a brick through the window.*

RIDING RIDDLES

A cyclist hired a tandem to go to a certain village and
back for £10. Halfway there he met a friend who wanted
to go to the same village and return to the halfway spot.
The friend agreed to pay a fair share of the hire charge.
How much should he pay?

Answer on page 151.

The number of people taking to two wheels in London soared by 83% over the seven years to 2007, due in no small measure to the introduction of congestion charging. But there is still room for improvement, perhaps along the lines of these cycle-friendly towns and cities across Europe:

Groningen, Netherlands: The capital of the Dutch province of Groningen is legendary for its proportion of bicycle traffic, which amounts to approximately 50% of all trips. This success is mainly due to restrictions for car traffic in the city centre, and the creation of a 200km network of cycle ways.

Trondheim, Norway: In addition to extensive cycle lanes, the city added a bicycle lift (like a coin-operated ski lift) to help cyclists up one particularly steep hill. The lift is 130m long, has a 1:5 gradient, and carries up to 300 cyclists per hour.

Odense, Denmark: The 'Green Wave', a novel use of automated lighting signals along the city's cycle ways, makes it possible for cyclists to pace their journey so they never have to stop at traffic lights.

Basel, Switzerland: Most one-way streets allow two-way bicycle traffic, and speed humps have flat passages for cyclists; at major intersections cyclists can use extra lanes for turning to the left and many bus lanes are open to cyclists.

Ferrara, Italy: Cycling really is a way of life here – Ferrara has 140,000 inhabitants and 110,000 bicycles. More than 30% of trips are made by bicycle. The town centre is pedestrianised, but accessible to cyclists. A large network of roads around the centre is open to car traffic, but with multiple restrictions aimed at improving access and safety for cyclists.

SANDY SYMPHONY

It was an extensive bicycle tour of the Algerian Sahara in 1908 that inspired Gustav Holst, best known as composer of *The Planets*, to compose the orchestral suite *Beni Mora*.

According to Holst expert Kenric Taylor the three-part suite was premiered in London in 1912, to the distaste of one critic who exclaimed: 'We didn't ask for Biskra girls!' Fellow English composer Ralph Vaughan Williams later said that if the exotic work had debuted in Paris instead of London, Holst would have gained fame a decade before *The Planets* made him a household name.

STAY PRESSED

If you commute to work, the easiest way to transport office clothes without too much creasing is to wear them. If you ride a long way, or like to push your pace, then you will no doubt prefer to change out of your sweaty cycle gear on arrival. Stowing your clothes does not mean stuffing them into the corner of your rucksack, however. If you want to avoid becoming known as the office scruff, follow these simple packing instructions to ensure your shirt, blouse or jacket does not get too creased:

1. Fasten the top and bottom buttons and place the garment front-down on a flat surface.

2. Fold in at the shoulders, laying the sleeves flat down the back of the shirt.

3. Gently roll from the tail to the shoulder panel, stopping at the back of the collar.

4. Place in a large padded envelope or carrier bag and stow in the top of your luggage where nothing will bear down on it.

5. Trousers should be folded in half at the knee – just where they are on the hanger – and then rolled. Pack them below the shirt, as they don't crease as easily.

LONG ARM OF THE LAW

In 1897, widespread interest in the cycling community and beyond was excited by the case of Mr Arthur Evans, a bootmaker from Liverpool, who was fined for 'furiously riding a bicycle'. The main facts of what came to be known as 'the Prescot hooking case' were that Mr Evans was riding down Prescot Brow, a steep gradient which, according to periodicals of the time, had become 'somewhat notorious in connection with cycling prosecutions'.

The novel and extraordinary feature of this case was that the accused man, while travelling at 'a terrific speed', was hooked under the arm and pulled off his machine by a policeman.

Mr Evans came to the ground with great force, and was severely bruised and cut – it was considered a marvel that he was not killed or crippled for life. A contemporary report wryly noted that 'he certainly would have been had he been riding at the speed alleged by the police... It is satisfactory to know that the Quarter Sessions Court has allowed his appeal in this case, and has thus done something to restore shattered public confidence in a fair and reasonable administration of the law as to cyclists.'

WRITERS ON BICYCLES

The perfected cyclist is a wondering spirit, full of eyes, like the beast in the Revelation. All the burden of humanity falls from him as he mounts. He has no past, neither does his future extend beyond the flying day. If he looks at all beyond the next turning, it is to the crowning satisfaction of supper.

JW Allen, *Wheel Magic and
Revolutions of an Impressionist*, 1909

QUOTE UNQUOTE

*Striking the right balance between caution and aggression
when riding through cities is the key to staying on your bike.
If you always assume that the car/lorry/motorbike in front
or behind of you is going to do the worst possible thing,
you give yourself a much better chance of staying alive.
However, knowing when to step up the pace to get yourself
out of trouble is also an important skill.*
James Daley, journalist, *The Independent*

BOARD RIDERS

For those rainy days when you really don't fancy getting in the saddle, there is a good selection of board games based on bicycle racing. The games listed below, and many more besides, can be found at www.boardgamegeek.com.

Breaking Away
For 2-9 players. Each player controls a team of four cyclists in a track race.

Um Reifenbreite
('By the Width of a Tyre')
For 2-4 players. You are in charge of a four-member team as it competes in the various stages of a grand tour.

6-Tage Rennen **('Six-Day Race')**
For 3-8 players. An attempt to recreate the thrill of an epic track race, turning cards instead of pedals to move forward.

The Official Tour de France Game
For 2-6 players. Published in 2003, the year the tour celebrated its 100th anniversary.

Breakaway Rider
For 2-6 players. Card-based game in which players compete for the yellow jersey in a race.

A Qui le Tour?
('Whose Turn is It?')
For 2-4 players. Each player controls a team of riders who must work together in order to be successful.

RIDING RIDDLES

Who is this famous cyclist?
ENTER COPERNICAN
Answer on page 151.

TO BATTLE ON A BIKE

Bicycles have often played a role in major conflicts.

Boer War

The first real testing ground for bicycles in war. Military cyclists were used primarily as scouts and messengers, though several raids were conducted on both sides by cycle-mounted infantry. The Royal Australian Cycle Corps built an eight-man tandem known as the 'war cycle', featuring detachable wheel rims, which could be adapted for use on the railroad.

World War I

An estimated 400,000 bicycle troops took part in the Great War. They were used by both sides, mainly for reconnaissance, communications and transporting infantry and supplies. There were also cycle-mounted commando units, able to move swiftly and silently under cover of darkness to carry out demolition raids behind enemy lines. In 1914, Germany's First Bicycle Company, Rifle Battalion, launched a surprise attack using bicycle-mounted machine guns and trailers full of dynamite to destroy the Marne River bridge at Mont-Saint-Père, France. The 200 cycle-borne troops outmanoeuvred the 4,000-strong defence force, killing more than 400 Frenchmen, while losing only five of their own men.

World War II

After deploying some 50,000 bicycle troops in its 1937 invasion of China, the Japanese Army used them extensively in its southern campaign through what was then Malaya, en route to capturing Singapore in 1941 – an event described by Winston Churchill as 'the worst disaster and largest capitulation in British history'. Allied use of the bicycle in World War II included supplying folding bicycles to paratroopers and to messengers behind friendly lines. The successful British raid on a German radar installation at Bruneval, France, in 1942 was conducted by airborne cyclist-commandos equipped with folding bikes.

Vietnam

The Vietcong used a massive fleet of bicycle couriers to supply its network of bases along the Ho Chi Minh Trail, creating a stealthy communications network that was largely unhindered by US air bombing. They also launched hundreds of bike-bomb attacks in Saigon.

Number of trips in millions made by riders using the National Cycle 117
Network in 2005 – a 41% increase from 2000

CYCLING WITH GUNS

Only in the US, it might be imagined, would readers of a cycling publication enter into a debate about the pros and cons of riding with a handgun. The following excerpts give a flavour of the correspondence on the subject that appeared in the September 2001 edition of the online journal cyclingnews.com.

'You should never carry a handgun unless you have the means to fully control it and I wouldn't believe anyone who told me they could do that and ride a bike. If you do get into a situation where you find a handgun is necessary, it would mean slowing down, getting off the bike, getting the gun out, and aiming it. Given that your adrenaline is probably pumping at this point, you'd most likely need to use two hands to control the gun.'
TL, September 11

'While in Cordoba [Argentina], I rode on several occasions with a fellow cyclist who was a police officer. As strange as it sounds, he had his gun (a 9mm) and holster under his jersey... We rode in the hills outside the city and through some very poor farming areas. Fortunately it was NEVER needed. When I asked my host father about it, he didn't seem to think it was too far from the norm.'
JB, Portland, Oregon, September 12

'I own a hand gun and live down on the border of Mexico in southern Arizona.'

I often ride alone through the mountains and roads that are notorious for drug runners. These people do not value human life. They are often looking for cars and bikes for transportation. Many people have been beaten and left for dead by these bandits. So I carry a gun. I know how to shoot...'
DW, Arizona, September 15

'I don't see why you can't control a gun on a bike – cowboys do it all the time on horseback... control the gun I mean.'
AL, September 15

'Try pepper spray or tear gas instead of a gun. I have used it in two instances with great results. They both reacted like they had been hit in the head with a sledgehammer. Although I felt guilty hosing down those people later, I did feel fully justified in defending myself from a lethal weapon – namely a car. It is a dual edge sword though, so be careful when using it because the spray can be blown back into your face.'
TF, September 16

OLD PICTURE, NEW CAPTION

Yet another of Harold's attempts at the 24-hour distance
record was scuppered by his insatiable thirst for beer.

SUICIDAL SQUIRREL

Finnish opera singer Esa Ruuttunen was once left concussed and
bleeding after a squirrel ran into his bicycle wheel. The leading
baritone was on his way to a rehearsal at the Helsinki Opera
House in September 2006 when the animal crashed into his
spokes. Ruuttunen was knocked out and ended up with a broken
nose, but recovered in time for the world premier of *Käärmeen
Hetki* ('Hour of the Serpent'). The squirrel died in the collision.

POPULAR LONG-DISTANCE CYCLE
ROUTES IN ENGLAND

The Marriott's Way

The Marriott's Way is long but flat, which makes for a good day's
riding if you are not feeling energetic enough for hill climbs. Named
after William Marriott, once chief engineer and manager of the
Midland & Great Northern Joint Railway, the secluded 21-mile
route runs along the former railway line between Hellesdon, on the
north-west fringe of Norwich, and Aylsham.

CYCLE HELMETS: THE LIMITATIONS ON LIDS

The main benefit of wearing a cycle helmet is the protection offered in the case of simple, 'low-impact' accidents, preventing injuries such as mild concussion and cuts to the scalp. However, many cycling organisations – including CTC, the UK's national cyclists' organisation – argue that any moves to make helmet-wearing compulsory would be counterproductive, and that the decision should rest with each rider. Here are some of the main reasons for that argument, as outlined by the CTC:

1. Cycle helmets offer limited protection and are only designed to absorb the impact of a fall at speeds up to 12.5mph.

2. Cycle helmets cannot offer adequate protection against the sort of impact that typically arises as a result of being struck by a motor vehicle travelling at speed.

3. No helmet has ever prevented a crash from occurring.

4. Helmets offer no protection to other parts of the body.

5. Insisting on the wearing of helmets may give the impression that cycling is more dangerous than it actually is and so deters potential cyclists.

6. An over-emphasis on helmet wearing encourages a culture in which the innocent victims of road crashes are blamed for their own injuries.

7. In countries where helmet use has been made compulsory there has been no corresponding decrease in injury rates or their severity, the main consequence being a large drop in the number of people cycling.

8. The use of helmets has been associated with a drop in the perceived vulnerability of cyclists on the part of other road users and on the part of cyclists themselves, so leading to an increase in risk-taking behaviour.

9. There is also some evidence that the wearing of a cycle helmet can make some form of head injury more likely, especially those caused by the brain rotating within the skull.

RIDING BACKWARDS

The one-hour record for riding backwards (pedalling while seated on the handlebars of a normal bicycle) was set on 24 May 2003, by Markus Riese, of Germany. He achieved a distance of 29.1km. He continued cycling until he broke the 50km backward-cycling record, recording a time of 1 hour, 46 minutes and 59 seconds.

120 *Time in minutes into every ride that a cyclist should eat a 'bonk bar' to avoid fatigue and sickness brought on by a lowering of blood sugar level*

BICYCLE ART

Some of the many works of fine art that feature bicycles

Henri de Toulouse-Lautrec – *La Chaine Simpson*, 1896 (one of many classic posters designed by the artist for manufacturers, in this case an advert for bicycle chains)

Marcel Duchamp – *Bicycle Wheel*, 1913 (bicycle fork and wheel screwed upside down onto a white stool)

Umberto Boccioni – *Dynamism of a Cyclist*, 1913 (oil painting in the Futurist style)

Max Ernst – *The Gramineous Bicycle Garnished with Bells the Dappled Fire Damps and the Echinoderms Bending the Spine to Look for Caresses*, 1920/1921 (a surreal painting every bit as strange as its title suggests)

Salvador Dalí – *Illumined Pleasures*, 1929 (a group of men riding bicycles feature in this visual record of a dream)

Max Oppenheimer – *Sechstagerennen*, 1929 (Futurist depiction of a six-day race at the Berlin Sportpalast)

Pablo Picasso – *Head of a Bull*, 1943 (sculpture, assemblage of bicycle seat and handlebars)

THE ICE MAN COMETH

It's not just present-day extreme sports fans that like to take the odd risk, as this 1879 letter to CTC's journal Cycling, *from A Montague Shepherd of the Kendal Amateur Bicycle Club, shows...*

On Saturday, December 20th, the ice on Grasmere Lake being in splendid condition, I thought I would try it instead of the frozen roads. So getting on to a piece of well-worn ice, where it was not slippy, I mounted, and was soon flying away, faster than on any bicycle track yet made, feeling not the slightest friction. I raced one or two fast skaters, but beat them easily...

On the following day I went again but hadn't gone a dozen yards when my front wheel caught against the side of a frozen ridge, and down I went like lightning and the bicycle on top of me. The results were a slightly sprained leg, and the left crank up nearly into the wheel.

I should think a fall going at a great pace would break some limb or limbs, but I am not dismayed, and if the front holds till Wednesday I am going to try and ride 100 miles in the eight hours... A good man on a racing machine could, I confidently assert, beat record times on the ice, and I strongly advise all riders to use this smooth path, this winter time, when the roads are either stony, rutty, or hard frozen.

TAKING YOUR BICYCLE ON THE TRAIN

Taking a bicycle is free on National Rail services, but any journey involving a bike will require a knowledge of the relevant operators' service restrictions and storage requirements – so be prepared to do your research and book well in advance*.

It is worth noting, however, that some operators have started offering extra services in a bid to become more cyclist-friendly. GNER, for instance, has introduced an online reservation system for bicycles (tandems count as two spaces), while First ScotRail and 'one' offer a 'cycle rescue' scheme for cyclists with a valid ticket: in the event of a breakdown, they will arrange to pick up the rider and their machine, then drop them at their nearest station, cycle repair shop or car rental agency (or even home, if it is the closest option).

If you prefer to leave your own bike at home, you will find cycle hire facilities available at an increasing number of stations, including Bath, York, Lancaster, Cromer and Cambridge.

* A leaflet summarising each train company's policy for carrying cycles is available from National Rail (visit: www.nationalrail.co.uk/passenger_services/cyclists.htm for a downloadable copy).

MOVING HOUSE

From time to time, everyone uses their bicycles to carry more than the usual load – bags stuffed with shopping, panniers full of camping equipment, or a child in a rear seat.

Long-distance cyclist and internet blogger Max Poletto went further than most, stretching the concept of 'utility cycling' to the limit. In June 2003, after finding that local removal firms were booked up, he used an 8ft-long trailer attached to the back of his bicycle to move his belongings over 7km to a new apartment in Cambridge, near Boston, Massachusetts. He made 13 trips with the trailer – an aluminium structure large enough to carry a bed and with a load capacity in excess of 300lb – covering a total distance of around 90km.

'In the end I only spent five hours actually cycling: packing, carrying things up and down stairs, and loading and unloading the trailer took more than twice that much time,' he wrote in an account of the big move. 'I finally own a real SUV: unlike the motorised ones, mine actually combines sport with utility.'

STEEP CLIMBS

Five UK roads that are likely to force all but the hardiest of hill climbers to do the unthinkable… dismount and push the bike up the hill.

Porlock Hill, Devon, England
Gradient of 1:4
Hairpin bends add to the difficulty, particularly on the scary, brake-melting descent from the heights of Exmoor.

Ffordd Penllech, Harlech, Gwynedd, Wales
Gradient of 1:2.5
The sign at the top of this winding stretch of road, marked unsuitable for motors, says '1 in 2.5'.

Hardknott and Wrynose passes, Lake District, England
Gradient of 1:3
Two tough climbs in quick succession for those who dare; a narrow and winding switchback road runs over each of the passes (both of which are 393m high at their peaks).

Bealach na Ba, Applecross Hills, West Highlands, Scotland
Gradient of 1:5
The road rises from sea level to an altitude of 626m in 10km. There's a cycle route which begins and ends at Torridon youth hostel, which makes an excellent base from which to tackle this epic climb.

Chimney Bank, Rosedale, North Yorkshire Moors, England *Gradient of 1:3*
Known as one of the most fearsome climbs in Britain, and regularly the site of cyclists' hill climb championships.

QUOTE UNQUOTE

The bicycle is the noblest invention of mankind.
William Saroyan, author, *The Bicycle Rider in Beverly Hills*

RIDING HIGH

The highest paved road in Britain, rising to 848m, is the private one leading to the gates of the radar station on Great Dun Fell in the Pennines.

The good news for cyclists with a penchant for tough climbs is that, while cars are barred, bikes are welcome, so you can enjoy spectacular views on a traffic-free route through the clouds.

WHAT THE DICKENS?

Pickwick Bicycle Club (Hackney, London) – founded 1870

The oldest cycling club in Britain was formed at the Downs Hotel on 22 June 1870, just days after the death of Charles Dickens. The building where that first meeting took place is marked by a historic plaque.

One of the most unusual aspects of the club is that its 200 members take sobriquets from characters in Dickens's novel *The Pickwick Papers*. As the club is an all-male preserve, even the female characters in the book are allotted to men. Membership is by invitation, and new places become available only when an existing member dies; prospective joiners generally face waits of up to seven years for an opening.

Members are mostly leading figures from the bike industry (the UK boss of Specialized, Richard Hemington, reportedly joined as 'the convict' in 1999), with a good smattering of high-profile city gents from the worlds of banking and law. The club organises rides at home and abroad, including one called 'Mr Pickwick Goes to France'.

But it could be argued that the main focus of activity is fine dining and hob-nobbing at the legendary bi-annual luncheons, at the New Connaught Rooms in London's Covent Garden, which members attend in the Pickwick uniform of brass name badge, straw boater and club tie.

One of the few insights into these secretive meetings for club members and their guests was given by Godfrey Smith, *Sunday Times* columnist, in 1995:

'I spent last Thursday in a time warp. The Pickwick Bicycle Club was holding its 125th anniversary lunch and, as befits the oldest bicycle club in the world and the oldest Dickensian association extant, did it in splendour. After the steak and kidney, the punch was ceremoniously wheeled in by two Chelsea pensioners while we sang 'The Boys of the Old Brigade'. Trumpeters of the Grenadier Guards serenaded us.

'A clay pipe and Pickwick shag was placed before every one of the 400 men there, for need I say this was a stag do, and indeed one of the most disgracefully politically incorrect rave-ups it has been my pleasure to attend for many a long year.

'David Mellor made a half-hour speech so packed with one-liners that I find myself unable to remember one. We staggered out into the brilliant sunshine not quite sure if it hadn't been a dream.'

Flying machine

Riding a bicycle at speed, downhill, is the closest many of us will come to the sensation of flying like a bird. But for some cyclists, that's not enough – they want to actually take off and fly. Enter the 'flying machine with helium-filled floating body and propeller, carrying a suspended pilot on a bicycle structure with steering and a propeller pedal drive'. Alas, vistas may be limited, as the

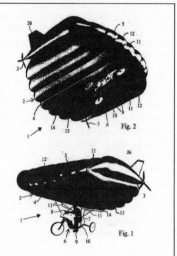

inventors suggest (perhaps wisely), that any flying should be done 'within enclosed halls and the like'.

Inventor: Guenter Mugrauer/Rainer Mugrauer (Germany)

Patent number: DE10150609, published April 2003

HAIRY RIDE

Corruption of various forms has always coloured professional cycle racing, and in the early days of the Tour de France it was not uncommon for riders to be attacked, or for nails to be placed on the roads and bikes sabotaged by fans or henchmen of rival competitors.

This resulted in some interesting survival tactics. In 1911, for instance, the race leader (and eventual winner), Gustave Garrigou, is said to have worn dark glasses and a false moustache for a stage in Rouen – the disguise was to help him evade a local lynch mob made up of supporters of his nearest rival.

EXTREME CYCLING

Bicycle mountaineering

Most cyclists see steep hill climbs as something to be avoided. Others don't like to get on their bikes at all unless they are faced with a near-vertical road to ascend. The main organisation for cycling's mountaineers in the UK is OCD CycloClimbing, a version of France's *Ordre des Cols Durs* ('the club of the hard cols').

Perhaps the single toughest challenge for climbers is that presented by the Hundred Cols Tour, a 4,000km ride over all the great mountainous areas of France, taking in 100 cols (mountain passes) in a month or more of daily rides. The annual event has been run since 1979 by a Dutch touring club, *Stichting Honderd Cols Tocht*

– somewhat perversely, one might think, considering the Netherlands is known for being so flat. But there are undoubtedly certain attractions to taking the high road by bike.

As the former secretary of OCD CycloClimbing, John Partington, put it: 'You leave the town far below, perhaps rise above the clouds. The weather changes: sun, shade, maybe even snow at the top. The breeze goes against you and then with you on the hairpins. At the top you have the view, and the mountain hospitality.' And then, unlike mountaineering, you have the reward of freewheeling all the way back downhill.

BAG A BIKING BUDDY

Cycling can sometimes seem a lonely activity. But you don't have to join your local cycling club to find someone to ride with. BikeBUDi is a free scheme that matches cyclists with others looking to travel in the same direction.

Once you register online at www.bikebudi.com and enter your journey details, possible matches are displayed on a local map, allowing you to easily identify suitable riding companions – whether for the commute to work or a weekend leisure ride.

The idea is not just to help current cyclists to find a bike buddy, but also to encourage individuals, who may have concerns about cycling, to give it a go by partnering more experienced riders.

The internet-based system also calculates the financial and CO_2 saving you could make compared to making that journey by car.

A DEATH AT THE RACES

Cyclists who have died or sustained fatal injuries during races

Francisco Cepeda, *Spain,*
Tour de France, 1935
Fell into a ravine on the
descent from Galibier;
died three days later.

André Raynaud, *France,*
racing in Belgium, 1937
Died during a race in Antwerp.

Serse Coppi, *Italy,*
Tour of Piedmont, 1951
Crashed within 1km of the
finish line. He completed the
race, but died hours later from
his injuries.

Russell Mockridge, *Australia,*
Tour of Gippsland, 1958
Killed in a collision with a bus
in Melbourne.

Tom Simpson, *United Kingdom,*
Tour de France, 1967
Suffered a fatal heart attack
while on the climb up
Mont Ventoux.

Jean-Pierre Monseré, *Belgium,*
Grand Prix Rétié, 1971
The 1970 World Champion was
hit by an oncoming car.

Manuel Galera, *Spain,*
Tour of Andalusia, 1972
Fell during a climb on the
second stage.

Juan Manuel Santisteban, *Spain,*
Giro d'Italia, 1976
Hit a guardrail early in the race
and was killed instantly.

Joaquim Agostinho, *Portugal,*
Tour of Algarve, 1984
Fell to the ground after colliding
with a dog.

Vicente Mata Ventura, *Spain,*
Luis Puig Trophy, 1987
Collided with a car.

Fabio Casartelli, *Italy,*
Tour de France, 1995
Fell with other riders on the
descent from Col de Portet
d'Aspet.

Manuel Sanroma, *Spain,*
Volta a Catalunya, 1999
Hit a barricade.

Saúl Morales, *Spain,*
Tour of Argentina, 2000
Hit by a lorry while on the
seventh stage.

Andrei Kivilev, *Kazakhstan,*
Paris-Nice, 2003
Died from head injuries
sustained during a crash.

Juan Barrero, *Colombia,*
Tour of Colombia, 2004
Fell during a high-speed descent.

Alessio Galletti, *Italy,*
Subida al Naranco, 2005
Suffered a fatal heart attack
during a climb.

Isaac Gálvez Lopez, *Spain,*
Ghent six-day race, 2006
Crashed into a railing after
colliding with another rider.

TEN CYCLING FIRSTS

• Scottish blacksmith Kirkpatrick Macmillan is credited with constructing the first pedal cycle in 1839.

• The first recorded bicycle race took place at the Parc Saint Cloud, Paris, in 1868.

• In 1888, CTC successfully lobbied for an Act of Parliament that established once and for all the legal status of the cycle.

• Cycling was included in the programme of the first modern Olympic Games in 1896.

• The first Tour de France was held in 1903.

• The use of rear lights on British roads became a legal requirement in 1945.

• Architect Eric Claxton designed Britain's first network of segregated cycle paths in 1946, as part of his plan for Stevenage New Town.

• The Tour of Britain was held for the first time in 1951.

• In 1955, Brian Robinson and Tony Hoar became the first British riders to complete the Tour de France.

• The first mass-produced mountain bikes were produced (by Specialized) in 1983.

ROAD HOG

In January 1895, a Bristol cyclist was awarded £30 damages, plus costs, in the Chippenham County Court, against a farmer who allowed his pigs to stray upon the highway 'so as to bring the rider and his machine to grief'.

WRITERS ON BICYCLES

Cyclists fight an ongoing war with guys in big trucks, and so many vehicles have hit me, so many times, in so many countries, I've lost count... One minute you're pedalling along a highway, and the next minute, boom, you're face-down in the dirt. A blast of hot air hits you, you taste the acrid, oily exhaust in the roof of your mouth, and all you can do is wave a fist at the disappearing taillights.

Lance Armstrong, *It's Not About the Bike: My Journey Back to Life*, 2001

THE CULT OF THE COURIER

Cycle couriers have been a part of city life for as long as the bicycle itself. The earliest messengers in London, Paris and New York, as depicted in grainy photographs from the 19th century, zipped about wearing caps, uniforms and spats, and tended to be young working-class boys.

Their modern counterparts are a more diverse bunch, of all ages and backgrounds, from resting actors to sons of wealthy lawyers, and they take pride in their profession despite the manifold risks; they are, in the words of *The Seattle Times*, 'toned, tattooed daredevils who cut through exhaust and traffic all day long'.

Many cities around the world have their own community of messengers, but the various tribes are united by a shared sense of identity, defined as much by courier culture and sport as the job itself. The ultimate global gathering is the Cycle Messenger World Championships (the 15th edition was held in Dublin in 2007).

The courier's machine is the first thing that sets him apart from other two-wheeled road users. Messengers favour a certain type of bicycle (fixed-wheeled, track racing frames, often decorated with strips of insulation tape over the maker's name) and a sporty riding position (high seat, low handlebars, in the style of a track racer). In recent years, these affectations have been much admired and imitated by other urban cyclists whom the couriers themselves refer to, somewhat disparagingly, as 'fakengers'.

BUILT FOR COMFORT AND SPEED

Recumbent riders are an exotic breed of cyclist, eyed with some suspicion by people who prefer more traditional, 'upright' bicycles. The bikes come in all shapes and sizes, from leisurely tandems to racing machines, and while they might draw some funny looks, their users are safe in the knowledge that their machines are (a) more comfortable and (b) generally more efficient than other pedal cycles.

In fact, despite their laid-back riding position, recumbents are so fast that in 1934 they were banned from competing against conventional bikes by cycle sport's governing body, the *Union Cycliste Internationale* (UCI). Not that that has stopped their riders from racing and breaking records – they have simply done so under the aegis of the Human Powered Vehicle Association (HPVA). The current world speed record, as recognised by the HPVA, was set by Sam Whittingham in 2007: he rode his Varna Diablo III at 53.917mph.

BIKE WEEK

Bike Week is the UK's annual celebration of cycling, with more than 1,500 local events attracting 250,000 participants. From easy, five-mile family rides on traffic-free routes to special breakfasts for cycling commuters, most Bike Week events are free to enter and suitable for cyclists of all abilities.

Bike Week and Bike2Work events and rides are listed at www.bikeweek.org.uk (or telephone 0845 612 0661 for details). Some Bike Week rides are to raise funds for good causes, including Bike Week's charity partner, Leukaemia Research.

Bike Week was started in 1923 by campaigners seeking to improve roads and facilities for cyclists. Now Bike Week is a government- and cycle industry-funded initiative designed to get 'more people cycling more often'. Event organisers range from cycling clubs and community groups to local councils and other major employers including NHS trusts, plus universities and schools.

RIDING RIDDLES

A cyclist left a café without paying, handing the cashier a slip of paper with these figures on it; 1004180. The cashier nodded and allowed her to pass – why?

Answer on page 151.

A STAR TURN FOR A CHAMPION RACER

Evelyn Hamilton began competing as an amateur in 1926 and won the 1931 cup for a half-mile sprint race at London's Stamford Bridge – the first of many victories she recorded in the 1930s. She later turned to endurance races, and the highlight of her career was a 100-day race in which she covered 12,800 miles.

When she wasn't racing, Hamilton also had a bike shop in Streatham, south London, where she built machines for professional riders.

In 1934, however, she was about as far removed from the race track or workshop as it's possible to get, appearing in a cycling scene in the film *Sing As We Go*, which starred Gracie Fields.

NAVAL MANOEUVRES

Brian Kilgannon, a member of the Royal Navy and Royal Marine Cycling Association, set a cycling record in 2007 without even leaving his ship. The Ministry of Defence Guard rode a distance of 1,017 miles in 60 hours on a stationary training bicycle.

His feat made it into *The Book of Alternative Records* as the record for 1,000 miles on a static bike. The name of the ship on which he set the record could not have been more apt: *HMS Raleigh*.

SEX AND CYCLING

Why cyclists make better lovers

The results of many scientific studies over the last decade have given male riders cause for concern, by linking cycling with erectile dysfunction and infertility. In 2000, for instance, Austrian researchers reported that 96% of mountain bikers they studied had experienced 'scrotal abnormalities' including calcium deposits, cysts and twisted veins – the latter of which are known to impair fertility. However, such evidence is counter-balanced by medical experts who promote cycling as a way of boosting health in general and sexual performance in particular. A study by the University of California at San Diego suggested that men who followed a regular exercise programme reported a 30% increase in frequency of sex with their partners and 30% more orgasms. Moreover, *Bicycling* magazine, a leading US publication, explained 'why cyclists make better lovers' by listing a number of sex-related benefits of riding, including:

• Greater blood circulation ('cycling helps build the cardiovascular system, which improves blood flow throughout the body and especially to the penis')
• Increased sexual endurance ('because cycling improves your cardiovascular conditioning, cyclists don't tire as quickly during lovemaking')
• Stronger sex muscles ('cycling improves your legs, buttocks, and lower-back muscles, all key muscles used during intercourse')
• Bigger sex organs ('cycling can reduce fat that builds up around the base of a man's penis. In essence, since this fat reduces penis size, cycling can make the penis look as large as possible')
• More endorphins ('regular exercise increases the body's release of endorphins, which has been shown to increase sexual arousal')

CYCLING FOR THE COMMON GOOD

An EU handbook aimed at encouraging more European towns and cities to promote more cycle use cited the following advantages for individuals and communities:

• Total lack of impact on the quality of life in the town (neither noise nor pollution)

• Preservation of monuments and planted areas

• Less space taken up on the ground, both for moving and for parking, and hence a more profitable use of the surface area

• Less deterioration to the road network and a reduction in the need for new road infrastructures

• Improvement to the attractiveness of town centres

• Fewer traffic jams and the economic losses that they entail

• The increased fluidity of car circulation

• The increased appeal of public transport

• Greater accessibility to urban services for the entire population

• Parents freed from the chore of transporting their children gain time and money

• Cyclists gain considerable time over short and medium distances

• Possible disappearance of the need for a second car for a household

(from Cycling: the way ahead for towns and cities)

THE 100 CLUB: CYCLING CLUBS
MORE THAN A CENTURY OLD

Leek Cyclists' Club (Leek, Staffs) was established in 1876 as the Leek & Moorland Bicycle Club. The founders were concerned with promoting self-discipline and pride in its members, and opted for a militaristic uniform and the election of a captain to ensure club rules were followed on all rides – a prolonged blast on the captain's whistle was the order to mount, two blasts warned riders they were bunched too closely together.

Main activity: time trials

Club colours: blue/yellow/white

132 *Number of days it took paraplegic John Ryan to complete a 5,400-mile trip across Canada on his specially adapted handcycle*

High-value results of recent auctions of rare
and collectible pedal cycles.

**Edward Schwinn's childhood
bicycle (1957)** £18,000
(Sotheby's, 1999)
A one-off bike made specifically
for Edward Schwinn, future
head of the Schwinn bicycle
empire and great-grandson of its
founder, Ignaz Schwinn.

Locomotive-drive bike (1890s)
£17,000 *(Sotheby's, 1999)*
Prototype bicycle with
locomotive drive (reciprocating
rods) instead of a chain linking
cranks to the rear hub.

**Giraffe lamplighter's
bicycle (1898)** £17,000
(Sotheby's, 2001)
Tall bicycle used in the late 19th
century to light gas street lamps.
Its seat is more than 7ft off the
ground, and its chain is more
than three times the length of a
conventional bicycle chain.

Otto dicycle (1879)
£15,000 *(Bonhams, 2007)*
Example of a type of a machine
that was briefly popular in the
late 19th century – dicycles
have two large wheels arranged
side by side (rather than in
line), with the rider seated
in between.

Carroll chainless (c.1897)
£14,500 *(Copake Auction, 2007)*
The drive mechanism consists of
two large, interconnected cogs,
in place of a chain.

Bowden Spacelander (1960)
£13,000 *(Sotheby's, 2000)*
Built by automotive designer
Benjamin Bowden, this red
moulded fibre-glass bicycle
was innovative and ahead
of its time – it has, in effect, a
monocoque design, preceding
the production of modern
carbon fibre frames by almost
30 years. Only 525 were made
in 1960; fewer than 40 are
known to exist today.

**Gormully & Jeffrey adult two-
track tandem (1891)** £11,700
(Copake Auction, 2007)
A tandem tricycle, with two
large wheels either side of the
riders, and a smaller wheel out
in front.

**Roadmaster Supreme boys'
bicycle (1937)** £6,500
(Copake Auction, 2007)
Streamlined, art-deco styling,
created by the noted Finnish
industrial designer and architect
Onnie Mankki.

**Coventry Machinists Company
'Club' front-drive safety
bicycle (1886)** £5,500
(Bonhams, 2005)
Featuring a 40in front wheel,
20in rear wheel, crescent rims
and 'cow-horn' bars with
pear handles. Unlike modern
bicycles, the pedals and chain
drive the front wheel rather
than the rear.

INDECENT EXPOSURE TO CARS

It is not difficult to think of reasons *not* to cycle naked. Top of the list is the horrendous thought of possible injuries in a fall. It's not just scraped elbows – there are many moving parts on a bike waiting to trap delicate parts of the human body.

But none of this deters thousands of cyclists around the world from taking part in naked bike rides as a form of mass protest.

The rides take place in cities in the US, UK and France at different times of the year (usually timed to coincide with warmer weather in each region, for obvious reasons).

The general concept is best left to the organisers of the World Naked Bike Ride to explain: 'We face automobile traffic with our naked bodies as the best way of defending our dignity and exposing the unique dangers faced by cyclists and pedestrians as well as the negative consequences we all face due to dependence on oil, and other forms of non-renewable energy.'

QUOTE UNQUOTE

If all feeling for grace and beauty were not extinguished in the mass of mankind at the actual moment, such a method of locomotion as cycling could never have found acceptance; no man or woman with the slightest aesthetic sense could assume the ludicrous position necessary for it.
Marie Louise de la Ramée (aka 'Ouida'),
author, *The Ugliness of Modern Life*

RIDING BIKES AND ROBBING TRAINS

Had Bruce Reynolds stuck to cycling, the Great Train Robbery might never have taken place.

Reynolds, mastermind of the 1963 heist, one of the 20th century's most spectacular crimes, grew up with a passion for cycling that never really left him.

In his teens, before he turned to crime, Reynolds was a member of De Laune cycling club in south London, going on 50-mile Sunday runs. He spent the money he earned from his paper round on a Bates cycle.

According to short film *Riding Bikes and Robbing Trains*, Reynolds' love of cycling never faded and, sentenced to 25 years imprisonment in 1968 (having spent five years on the run), one of the things that kept him going in maximum security was the dream of riding through France with his son, Nick, who had grown up while he was in prison.

BIDLAKE MEMORIAL – CELEBRATING BRITISH GREATS

The Bidlake Memorial Prize, a prestigious annual award for British cyclists, was instituted in memory of Frederick Thomas Bidlake (1867-1933) – an English racing cyclist who went on to be a leading administrator of the sport. The list of past winners reads like a who's who of British cycling legends, and includes:

Hubert Opperman (first winner, 1934) Record-breaking long-distance cyclist

George Herbert Stancer (1943) Campaigning journalist and a president of CTC, then known as the Cyclists' Touring Club

Reg Harris (1947 and 1949) The first Englishman to win the Professional Sprint Cycling Championship of the World

Beryl Burton (1959, 1960 and 1967) Dominated women's cycle racing for many years, with records and championships galore

Tom Simpson (1965) The first British rider to win the Professional Road Race Championship of the World

Hugh Porter (1968) World Champion of the 5,000m individual pursuit

Chris Boardman (1992) Olympic gold medallist and breaker of the hour record

Graeme Obree (1993) Pursuit champion and hour-record challenger

Sean Yates (1994) Topped his racing career when he became the third Briton to wear the leader's yellow jersey in the Tour de France

Nicole Cooke (2001) Junior road and mountain biking champion who has since gone on to become a world beater in women's cycle sport

WRITERS ON BICYCLES

As a social revolutionizer, the bicycle has never had an equal. It has put the human race on wheels, and thus changed completely many of the most ordinary processes and methods of social life. It is the great leveler, for not till all Americans got on bicycles was the great American principle that every man is just as good as any other man fully realized. All are on equal terms, all are happier than ever before.

Anon, *New York Evening Post,* **1896**

WRITERS ON BICYCLES

Early cycling clubs and the 'Great Unattached'

In the early days of the wheel the club was a regular institution, which every rider felt bound to join. In fact, to be a member of the 'Great Unattached' was considered almost a disgrace, leading others to assume that the rider was not of sufficient respectability to become a member. The club uniform was as it were a Masonic sign, which acted as an introduction on the road. A rider attired in one of the well-known uniforms worn by the Stanley, London or Pickwick Clubs was considered a desirable acquaintance when met on a touring expedition. The early days of cycling were, to my way of thinking, far more pleasant and sociable than those in which we live now. Owing to the scarcity of riders every one felt bound by a common bond to assist a brother cyclist in distress for the common good of the sort. Many a score of pleasant evenings have I spent in the company of perfect strangers, whom I have joined on my wanderings, and whose sole introduction was a recognized club uniform. *Nous avons changé tout cela*! and the club uniform is no more. Worse still, nearly all the old clubs are dead.

Where is the Pickwick, the father of clubs; the Clarence, to whom Wat Britten belonged in the days of his famous record to Bath and back; and the Druids? All dead or practically defunct. A few of the old clubs still exist. Of these the London is an example; but as a rule ninety-nine out of every hundred of those who once attended on Hampton Court Green are no more, and their members are scattered over the wide world. What a wonderful thing we used to think our annual meet! How our club captains used to strive to bring every and all of our members to the great muster! The function was originally started as a sort of demonstration to show the outside public that cyclists – or, as we were then called, bicyclists – were more numerous and powerful than our opponents would have men believe. Union was our strength, and in the palmy days of Mr Paget, the anti-cycling magistrate at the Hammersmith police court, every effort had to be made to prevent the devotees of the wheel being unfairly treated and the sport killed by vexatious regulations.

AC Pemberton,
The Complete Cyclist, 1897

RIDING RIDDLES

Who is this famous cyclist?
BURLY BRETON
Answer on page 151.

*Percy realised it had been a big mistake
to run over the witch's foot.*

CRITICAL MASS

Critical Mass rides, which typically take place on the last Friday of every month in cities across the world, bring together riders of every hue – from white-collar commuters to militant activists – in a show of cycling solidarity.

For some, the rides are an overtly political demonstration against the car, and in favour of the bicycle and other eco-friendly transport solutions. Others see Critical Mass more as a celebration of cycling: a party on wheels complete with mobile (pedal-powered) sound systems.

The processions are generally peaceful affairs, although clashes with motorists have occurred – most notably in San Francisco, which happens to be where Critical Mass began in 1992, as a local event with around 50 riders. Since then, tens of thousands of cyclists have taken part in hundreds of Critical Mass rides around the world.

Reported number of naked, body-painted cyclists who took part in the 18th Annual Summer Solstice Parade & Pageant through Seattle in 2005 137

WRITERS ON BICYCLES

What a wonderful thing is the modern cycle! In years to come, when the historian writes of the Victorian age, he will, without doubt, feel himself constrained by the force of circumstances to write at length of the genesis and development of 'the bicycle' – that curious vehicle which in the nineteenth century added new and altogether unequalled powers of locomotion to those already possessed by man, powers which were dependent on man's muscles alone, and which enabled him to travel farther and faster than he has before been able to progress by their use.

George Lacy Hillier, *All Round Cycling*, 1899

FEET DON'T FAIL ME NOW

For the purposes of everyday cycling most riders stick with straightforward 'platform' pedals. Others prefer pedals fitted with toe clips and straps (also known as 'cages'), or the more modern 'clipless' style of pedals used by racers. Fixing your feet to the pedals with either method allows you to pull up as well as push down, thus increasing the power with each stroke.

Clipless pedals work by means of a cleat attached to the bottom of the rider's shoe. Pushing down with your feet locks the cleats into a sprung mechanism on the pedal. To release the shoe from the pedal, the rider twists their heel to one side, forcing the cleat out of the spring. Clipless pedals can be tricky to use at first, and riders must be careful to adjust the spring tension: too loose and the shoes will keep coming away from the pedal, too tight and a rider could find themselves toppling over at the lights as they realise they can't pull their feet free.

Pedals with toe clips are platform pedals with a curved piece of plastic attached to the front to hold the rider's toe in place. A strap passes over the top of the rider's toes to secure the foot in place. As with clipless pedals, there is a learning curve: you have to get the hang of getting your feet in and out of the clips quickly, especially if you are forced to stop suddenly.

The only way to find out which system suits you – or if you should stick with the platform pedals that were attached to the bike when you bought it – is to try them. Before doing so, make sure you seek advice on fitting from your local bike shop.

TEN AMAZING FACTS ABOUT CYCLING

As compiled by Somerset County Council

• On a bicycle you can travel up to 1,037km on the energy equivalent of a single litre of petrol.

• On a bicycle you can expect to be as fit as an average person 10 years younger, if you cycle regularly.

• On a bicycle you weigh about six times more than your vehicle. In a car your vehicle weighs about 20 times more than you do.

• On a bicycle you provide the motor – your heart – which improves its own strength and efficiency, and even its working life, the more it is used.

• On a bicycle you can have your cake and eat it. A moderate half-hour each-way commute will burn eight calories a minute, or the equivalent of 11kg of fat in a year. Coasting at 3mph burns two calories a minute.

• On a bicycle you use up fewer watts of energy that a car consumes simply to power its lighting system for the same distance.

• On a bicycle, the exercise you do protects you against heart disease, high blood pressure, obesity and stress.

• On a bicycle you consume a fiftieth of the oxygen consumed by a motor vehicle, and expel no pollutants.

• On a bicycle you can travel four times faster than you can walk using the same amount of energy.

THE 100 CLUB: CYCLING CLUBS MORE THAN A CENTURY OLD

Oxford University Cycling Club, founded 1873, was originally known as the Dark Blue CC, which is now the name of the cyclist alumni club. Members compete in an annual varsity match against Cambridge – the cycling equivalent of the Boat Race. According to club records, an OUCC attendant was employed in the early years to clean its members' machines.

Main activities: road racing, time trialling, hill-climbing and mountain biking

Club colours: Blue

Famous members: Jim Henderson (member 1994-1998), five times winner of the British hill-climb championship.

Number of bicycles in thousands imported to the UK from India 139
in 2002

EXTREME CYCLING

Municycling

The emerging sport of municycling is mountain biking with one very important omission: a wheel. Mountain unicycling, to give it its full name, requires great fitness, strength and balance; imagine riding up a 30-degree bank, hopping over logs and rocks all the way, on one wheel. That's what municyclists do on a typical off-road trail. They also indulge in a fair bit of street riding, pulling tricks that appear to cross BMX with circus clowning; bound to bring smiles to the face of even the most surly of passing motorists.

Municycles are equipped with stronger hubs and frames, and fatter tyres, than normal unicycles. They also have a handle at the front of the seat to help the rider 'hop' and to aid stability. The best-known mountain unicyclist is the Canadian Kris Holm, winner of the European, North American and World Trials Championships.

ORCHESTRAL MANOEUVRES
IN THE MALVERNS

The composer Edward Elgar was a keen cyclist as well as brilliant musician. He was 43 when he first started cycling in 1900, spending £21 on a Royal Sunbeam fixed-wheel model with hand-polished black enamel finish. He toured extensively in the Malvern Hills, the rolling countryside surrounding his birthplace of Lower Broadheath, Worcestershire.

According to the Elgar Society, his wife Alice never really mastered the art so Elgar was often accompanied on his cycling trips by friends. One of them, Rosa Burley, recalled: 'Our cycling trips began in earnest after *Gerontius*... There cannot have been a lane within 20 miles of Malvern that we did not ultimately find... to Upton, to Tewkesbury or Hereford, to the Vale of Evesham... to the lovely village on the west side of the hills... as we rode, he would often become silent and I knew that some new melody or, more probably, some new piece of orchestral texture, had occurred to him.'

Though none of Elgar's bicycles appear to have survived, some of his cycling maps have, complete with the routes he carefully filled in, and his journals note how his cycling experiences had inspired many of his compositions.

ROCK 'N' ROLLERS

Musicians with a link to cycling

Eric Clapton – Owns several racing machines, and the name of the Cream album *Disraeli Gears* reputedly came from a roadie's slip of the tongue when talking about bikes: he had been meaning to say 'derailleur gears'.

Syd Barrett (Pink Floyd) – The famous recluse was spotted cycling around Cambridge in the years after he gave up his music career. His two, hand-painted bicycles (with baskets) were sold at auction after his death.

Sheryl Crow – Famously took to cycling after her relationship with Lance Armstrong.

Kraftwerk – Fanatical cyclists who devoted an album to the Tour de France and formed their own cycling club, *Radsportgruppe Schneider* ('The Schneider Cycling Club' – named after founding member Florian Schneider).

The Grateful Dead – The band rents studio space from Californian bike company Marin and guitarist Bob Weir, a keen mountain biker who rides with Gary Fisher (one of the founding fathers of the sport), was quoted as saying: 'Bicycles are almost as good as guitars for meeting girls.'

Jarvis Cocker – Was reportedly forced to give up cycling when he moved to Paris, due to the driving habits of the French.

Paul McCartney – Took over as patron of the Linda McCartney Pro Cycling Team following his first wife's death in 1998.

Madonna – Told *Vogue* magazine in 2007 that cycling was her preferred way of getting around London.

David Byrne (Talking Heads) – Travels around New York City on a mountain bike.

Mick Jagger – One of several celebrity customers of the British bike building firm Condor. He owns a racer and a custom hybrid.

Pete Shelley (The Buzzcocks) – Composed the synthesiser-heavy theme tune for Channel 4's Tour de France coverage in the 1990s.

RIDING RIDDLES

Two cyclists who live 84 miles apart start out at 9am to meet each other. One of them is travelling 12mph the other at 9mph, what time is it when they meet?

Answer on page 151.

Track racing

The place of Olympic and World Championship track racing is on a velodrome – an oval, 250m track with a smooth hardwood surface, and steeply banked curves to keep the riders from sliding out as they corner at high speed. Track cyclists, like sprint runners, are powerfully built athletes, and often rely on short, explosive bursts of speed to win races.

Their machines are stripped of all but the most essential equipment to ensure minimum weight and maximum aerodynamics: they have a single fixed gear and no brakes, and disc wheels. The main track disciplines are sprint and endurance. Events can take the form of head-to-head matches, with riders starting together, or pursuits, where riders start on opposite sides of the track and the fastest rider wins, unless one rider is caught by the other, at which point the race is over.

The initial stages of a sprint race can bemuse first-time spectators: riders often go at an extremely slow pace, perhaps even coming to a standstill (a 'track stand') as they jostle for the best position from which to launch their final attack. The winner often comes from behind, getting a 'tow' on the front rider's slipstream before pulling away with a sprint for the finish line.

The Keirin (Japanese for 'fight') is a track race in which several riders sprint for the finish after completing a series of laps behind a 'derny' (powered cycle) pacer. The derny gradually builds up speed, with riders jockeying for position behind, until it pulls off the track with two and a half laps to go – from then on it's a free-for-all to the line. Tactical and often very physical, with frequent crashes in the final sprint, Keirin makes for a bizarre but highly entertaining spectator event. It is hugely popular in Japan, where vast sums of money are gambled on the sport.

In time trials, riders compete individually against the clock to record the fastest time over the specified distance (or time) from a standing start. The records for 'the hour' and the 1,000m ('kilo') time trials are among the most highly prized goals in the sport.

QUOTE UNQUOTE

Let a man find himself, in distinction from others, on top of two wheels with a chain – at least in a poor country like Russia – and his vanity begins to swell out like his tyres. In America it takes an automobile to produce this effect.
Leon Trotsky, Bolshevik revolutionary,
The History of the Russian Revolution

NICKNAMES OF FAMOUS RIDERS

Claudio Chiappucci –
Il Diabolo (for his
reckless, attacking style
in the mountains)

Mario Cipollini – *Super Mario*
(for his big personality and
massive haul of victories –
191 wins in a career spanning
16 years)

Roger de Vlaeminck –
The Gypsy (he came from a
travelling family)

Charly Gaul – *Angel of the
Mountain* (because of his
climbing prowess)

Miguel Indurain – *Big Mig*
(for his stature, both physical
and as a race winner)

Bernard Hinault – *Le Blaireau*
('the badger', for his tough
fighting style when cornered)

Fausto Coppi –
Il Campionissimo ('The
Champion of the Champions'),
one of the most successful and
most popular cyclists of all time)

Laurent Fignon –
Le Professeur (he wore
glasses and had an
academic background)

Eddie Merckx – *Le Cannibale*
(because he devoured
everyone else on the road)

Marco Pantani –
Il Elefantino (because of his
prominent ears)

Djamolidine Abdoujaparov –
The Tashkent Terror (for his
ferocious sprinting style)

Graham Obree –
The Flying Scotsman (because
he was fast – and Scottish)

THE RISE OF A MONGREL BREED

One of the biggest changes in everyday cycling in recent years has
been the mass shift to so-called 'hybrid' bikes, which are
increasingly favoured by cycle commuters over mountain bikes.

According to a 2005 report by research company Mintel,
mountain bike sales slid from 50% of the market in 2000 to just
over 30% in 2004.

Meanwhile, there has been a dramatic growth in sales of
'hybrids', which generally feature a robust, mountain bike-style
frame with road bike features such as faster, 'skinny' tyres. Sales of
this type of machine soared from just 2% to 25% of the market in
the same period.

The Mintel study concludes that the trend is set to continue,
because it appears that 'cyclists are now buying more for function
than fashion'.

PEOPLE POWER

A few significant milestones along the road to human-powered transport

Prehistory: Rollers and runners
Early man places rollers (logs laid side-by-side) or runners (sledges) beneath heavy objects to move them more easily.

3,500BC: The earliest wheels
An etching from ancient Mesopotamia shows a sledge equipped with wooden wheels made from carved planks.

2,000 BC: Spoked wheels
Wooden spokes, developed in order to lighten the wheel, are used on chariots in Asia Minor. Refinements include iron hubs turning on greased axles and the introduction of iron tyres.

200BC-200AD: Pushing progress
The Chinese invent the wheelbarrow for use in warfare and agriculture, allowing individuals to move heavy goods without the need for horses.

1700-1800: Roller-skating
The invention of roller-skates is credited to Joseph Merlin, a Belgian, in 1760, though early models derived from ice-skates are reported in the early 1700s.

1817: The running man
In Germany, Baron Karl Drais von Sauerbronn invents the two-wheeled 'running machine', more commonly known in England as the hobby horse. It has steering but no pedals; the rider propels himself by scooting his feet along the ground.

1839: Forging ahead
Scottish blacksmith Kirkpatrick Macmillan is credited with constructing the first pedal cycle, based on the discovery that two wheels placed in line could be balanced while being propelled by means of rods connected to treadle-type pedals.

1861-1870: Boneshakers
Pierre Michaux adds cranked pedals to the front wheel of the hobby horse so the rider can propel himself without touching the ground. The invention is known in England as a 'boneshaker' because of its punishing lack of suspension.

1870-1895: High-wheelers
Makers soon realise that enlarging the front wheel results in a smoother, faster ride, leading to the development of the 'ordinary' bicycle, or penny farthing.

1885-1899: Safe at last
The revolutionary 'safety bicycle', featuring differential gears, a chain-driven rear wheel, and tangentially-spoked, similar-sized wheels, is produced in England. Further refinements before the end of the 19th century include pneumatic tyres and derailleur gears – the modern bicycle is born.

THE PUNCTURE BY W HEATH ROBINSON

WRITERS ON BICYCLES

That cycling produces important effects, both for good and evil, on the physical and moral well-being of women and children can scarcely be questioned... I have confined the age for cycling with impunity or benefit [to women] to between sixteen and forty. My reasons for this are these: before the former the bones are not sufficiently ossified to bear the strain to the spine and lower extremities involved in that form of exercise, and after the latter women suffer from the effects of fatigue to a greater extent than formerly. I have frequently noticed what I may define as the 'ravages' of cycling on women about that time of life. I have seen them rapidly decline in their 'good looks', become thin and wrinkled, and quickly lose any freshness of appearance they might have had previously.

J Beresford Ryley MD,
The Dangers of Cycling for Women and Children, **1899**

Typical diameter in centimetres of an 'ordinary' bicycle (or penny 145
farthing) front wheel in the late 1870s

EARLY CYCLING DITTIES

There once was a mechanician, who escap'd from a retreat,
Where the Lunacy Commissioners had bade him rest his feet;
He sought to cut the carriage out, to supercede the train –
And the cycle was the product of that mechanician's brain.

There was nought could stand against it, not the murder of the day,
The sensational divorce case, or the dullest problem play;
It drove the cabmen drinkwards, and it laughed the 'bus to scorn,
And it drowned the barrel organ with the music of its horn.

By pneumatic aid untyred doth the priest his circuit go,
And the azure-blooded peeress scorches madly down the Row;
The encyclopedic statesmen from 'The House' an hour steals,
And simultaneously revolves his speeches and his wheels.

Let the poet on his Safety his divine ideas review,
And the course of love run smoothly on a bicycle for two;
Let the tandem bear the parents, and you save a bassinette,
For the other olive branches to follow on a quadruplet.

May the wheels be never lessened, and thy tyres ne'er increased,
Thou shalt still be King, oh cycle, when the motor-car has ceased;
Still though I am unwilling thy exuberance to baulk,
Leave a corner of existence for the man who'd rather walk.

AW Skelton (lyrics), *The Cycling Fever*, c.1910

ON GOSSAMER WINGS

In 1979, Bryan Allen, amateur racing cyclist and self-taught hang glider, took off in a pedal-powered aircraft named the *Gossamer Albatross*, completing the first human-powered flight from England to France. He used pedals to drive a large, two-bladed propeller and completed the 22-mile crossing in 2 hours 49 minutes, achieving a top speed of 18mph and an average altitude of 5ft.

The *Albatross*'s inventor, Paul MacCready, was awarded the £100,000 Kremer prize for the first human-powered flight across the English Channel, established in 1959 by the industrialist Henry Kremer and administered by the Royal Aeronautical Society.

THE 100 CLUB: CYCLING CLUBS MORE THAN A CENTURY OLD

De Laune (Herne Hill, London) was founded in 1889 as the De Laune Institute Cycling Club, part of a network of social and sporting groups for young men set up by Chapman Delaune Faunce, High Sheriff of Kent and local landowner, in the parish of St Mary's, Newington, east London (the original home of the cycling club).

Main activities: time trials, track and road racing, and mountain biking

Club colours: blue/white

Famous members: Brian Dacey established himself as one of Britain's best veteran track racers, winning World Championship pursuit and points events in the 65-plus age category for two years running (2003-2004).

IT'S A WHEEL HONOUR

People who have been awarded honorary OBE or MBE awards for services to cycling:

Bradley Wiggins OBE
Olympic and world track racing champion

Ted King MBE
Ex-CTC president, who received his MBE for over 50 years' service to cycling

David Higman MBE
Cycle historian and founder of the National Cycle Museum

David Brailsford MBE
British Cycling's performance director

Phil Liggett, MBE
Television commentator and former CTC president

Chris Hoy MBE
Track cyclist – Olympic gold and silver medal winner

Tom Lynch MBE
Former UK and Euro BMX racing champion, who set up the first Cycle Response Unit (CRU) in the UK in 2000 for the London Ambulance Service

Chris Boardman MBE
Former Olympic and World Champion

Hugh Porter MBE
Former world champion (pursuit) turned BBC commentator

Aileen Mcglynn MBE
Gold medal-winning paralympian

Derek Roberts MBE
Founder member of the Veteran Cycling Club and the Fellowship of Cycling Old-Timers

Mountain Madonna

There are many sanctified stops for the cycling pilgrim, but the holiest of wheeling holies must surely be the Santuario della Madonna del Ghisallo, a 17th-century chapel at the top of a mountain road overlooking Lake Como in Italy.

The founding legend tells of a local aristocrat, the Count of Ghisallo, who sought divine protection at a roadside shrine after being set upon by bandits. The count was saved after seeing an apparition of the Virgin Mary, built a church in her honour, and the 'mountain Madonna' was thus established as a patron saint of travellers in the region.

In 1948, the rector, Don Ermelindo Viganò, persuaded Pope Pius XII to dedicate the building to cyclists, based on the chapel's association with Italian road racing (the Giro d'Italia and Giro di Lombardia regularly passed by). One year later, during the 1949 Giro d'Italia, the Pope made the Madonna patron saint of Italian riders.

Ever since, the chapel has been part shrine, part cycling museum, and a place of pilgrimage for thousands of riders every year. In recent years, however, the cornucopia of cycle sport paraphernalia that adorned the walls – World Champions' jerseys, race-winning bikes of legendary riders such as Fausto Coppi, Tour posters, photographs and pennants – began to overwhelm the tiny chapel, and local authorities decided to re-house the collection in a purpose-built museum.

The glass, steel and wood structure of the new Museo del Ciclismo, which stands adjacent to the Santuario, was officially opened on 14 October 2006, at the start of that year's Giro di Lombardia .

The museum boasts 2,000m^2 of floor space for travelling and permanent exhibitions, and recent additions include Danilo Di Luca's 2005 ProTour Champion jersey.

The new building has been blessed by Pope Benedict XVI, but – splendid as it is – has not diminished the Santuario's importance as a place of pilgrimage. Riders of all faiths (or none) continue pedalling up the Passo del Ghisallo to pay tribute, and most come away with the same saintly souvenir: a double-sided silver pendant depicting the Madonna with child, and on the reverse a cyclist with the chapel in the background.

Rigged exercise bikes to a generator and pedalled while we worked to power our computers, printers and the coffee machine.

Burned more than 5,000 calories a day (the same amount needed to sustain a Tour de France cyclist) while riding/writing on our exercise bikes.

Consumed more than 450 Mars bars, 600 litres of banana milkshake and 250 bowls of cereal over three months in a largely successful bid to beat 'the bonk'.

Spent most lunchtimes sleeping, or trying to persuade colleagues to massage our aching calves with oil.

Took to shaving and oiling our legs, just like the pros, and collected the hair for composting.

Called at least one bicycle courier to the office every day, even when we had nothing to despatch, so we could ask them annoying questions such as: 'Why hasn't your bike got gears?'

Raced children's trikes around the office velodrome (aka the canteen). Like any tough race, there were some nasty spills – mostly of nonplussed colleagues' coffee.

Experimented with several banned, performance-enhancing substances in order to complete the book to deadline (and cut time off the journey to work). Found that a daily dose of Marmite gave us a definite edge, though friends questioned the need to smear it all over our bodies for increased aerodynamism.

Practised taking apart our bicycles and putting them back together, while blindfolded. The best recorded time was 2 minutes 45 seconds, although few of the components were in the right place and we had to call in a bike mechanic before we were able to ride home.

Please note that although every effort has been made to ensure the accuracy of this book, the above facts may be the result of too much pedalling, punctures (and subsequent pushing)

Life is like a 10-speed bicycle.
Most of us have gears we never use.
Charles M Schulz

ANSWERS

The answers. As if you needed them.

P16   Chris Boardman

P21   Gears

P30   Floyd Landis

P34   Critical mass

P45   Lance Armstrong

P53   Marco Pantani

P60   Tyre

P71   The distance is 60 miles. If he left at noon and rode at 15mph he would arrive at 4pm – an hour too soon. If he rode at 10mph he would arrive at 6pm – an hour too late. But if he rode at 12mph he would arrive at 5pm, the appointed time.

P74   Miguel Indurain

P86   Spoke

P93   Cyclist B catches up with cyclist A at 11.45pm.

P101 By standing the signpost so that the proper arm pointed back to the village from which he had cycled, the other three arms then point in their right directions.

P113 As the friend has to pay only half the hire charge for half the distance, the answer is half of £5, which is £2.50.

P117 Connie Carpenter

P130 Because the cashier read the figure as: 'I owe nothing for I ate nothing'.

P136 Beryl Burton

P141 1pm

152 *Number of Dutch riders who won a stage in the Tour de France between 1903 and 2005*

BIBLIOGRAPHY

BOOKS

Bike Cult, David Perry

One More Kilometre and We're in the Showers, Tim Hilton

Cycle History 15 – Proceedings of the 15th International Cycling Conference, Andrew Ritchie and Nicholas Clayton (eds)

The Literary Cyclist, James E Starrs

Guinness Book of Cycling Facts and Feats, Jeremy Evans

The Birth of Dirt, Frank Berto

Extreme Sports, Joe Tomlinson and Ed Leigh

The History and Development of Cycles, CF Caunter

The First Century of the Bicycle and its Accessories, Lionel Joseph

Bicycling Science, David Gordon Wilson

Bicycles & Tricycles: A Classic Treatise on Their Design and Construction, Archibald Sharp

Pedal Power, James C McCullagh

Push Yourself Just a Little Bit More, Johnny Green

It's Not About the Bike: My Journey Back to Life, Lance Armstrong

Team on the Run, John Deering

Bikie: A Love Affair with the Racing Bicycle, Charlie Woods

The Rider, Tim Krabbé

The Complete Cyclist, AC Pemberton

Wheel Magic and *Revolutions of an Impressionist*, JW Allen

All Round Cycling, George Lacy Hillier

ACKNOWLEDGEMENTS

We gratefully acknowledge permission to reprint extracts of
copyright material in this book from the following authors,
publishers and executors:

It's Not About The Bike: My Journey Back to Life, Lance Armstrong
Published by Yellow Jersey Press. Reprinted by permission of The
Random House Group Ltd.

The Man Who Invented Sin, Sean O'Faolain
Published by Constable. Reprinted by permission of Rogers,
Coleridge & White Ltd.

The Rider, Tim Krabbé
Reprinted by kind permission of Bloomsbury Publishing.

Cakes and Ale, W Somerset Maughan
Published by William Heineman Ltd. Reprinted by permission of
The Random House Group Ltd.

The Puncture (illustration), WH Robinson
Reproduced by permission of Pollinger Limited and the proprietor.

The Ten Commandments of Cycling, Anthony Robson
– www.citycycling.co.uk

Portraits from Memory and Other Essays, Bertrand Russell
Published by Spokesman Books. Reprinted by kind permission of
The Bertrand Russell Peace Foundation.

An Unsocial Socialist, George Bernard Shaw
Reprinted by kind permission of 1st World Publishing.

Hovel in the Hills, Elizabeth West
Published by Faber and Faber Ltd. Reprinted by kind permission of
Elizabeth West.

Line drawings by Frank Patterson copyright of CTC. Reproduced
by kind permission of the CTC archive: p15, p25, p29, p41, p48,
p61, p71, p77, p95, p103, p113, p119.

INDEX

CTC – THE UK'S NATIONAL CYCLISTS' ORGANISATION; THEN AND NOW

There are few organisations that reach the age of 129 years, and fewer still with the fascinating history of CTC – the UK's national cyclists' organisation, which was founded in 1878.

It is thought that cycle touring was born in 1869 when two men cycled from Mersey to London. Bicycles were incredibly rare at that time, and travelling on Ordinary (penny-farthing) bicycles, the pair proved an astonishing sight to passers-by along the entire length of their journey.

As the activity became more popular, the need for an organisation to represent cycling grew. In 1878, a young gentleman called Stanley Cotterell formed a club which offered a defence on behalf of members involved in accidents, route information, companions for tours and recommendations on good hotels – all services that CTC still offers today.

Cycling continues to provide a healthy, cost-effective and environmentally friendly means of transport, and CTC has evolved to meet the needs of the modern cyclist.

Whether you are interested in cycling with your family at weekends, commuting to work by bike or a three-week cycling expedition in New Zealand, CTC can help. From getting you started with advice on what bike to buy and great deals on insurance through to training courses to help build your confidence on and off-road, CTC has become the essential accessory for all cyclists. In addition, we have an entire department dedicated to campaigning on behalf of cyclists' rights.

Join CTC, and in addition to supporting our work, you'll receive:
- Our award-winning bi-monthly magazine, *Cycle*
- Access to a huge collection of information on cycle routes and a helpline offering advice on all cycling matters
- An invitation to join local groups and a choice of thousands of rides and events
- £5 million third-party insurance and free legal advice
- Discounts on bicycles, accommodation, accessories and travel

To find out more, visit **www.ctc.org.uk**
or call 0870 873 0060